History

of the
Town of Plainfield

Hampshire County, Mass.
from Its Settlement to 1891

Including a Genealogical History of Twenty-three of
the Original Settlers and Their Descendants,
with Anecdotes and Sketches

by

Charles N. Dyer

HERITAGE BOOKS
2024

HERITAGE BOOKS
AN IMPRINT OF HERITAGE BOOKS, INC.

Books, CDs, and more—Worldwide

For our listing of thousands of titles see our website
at
www.HeritageBooks.com

A Facsimile Reprint
Published 2024 by
HERITAGE BOOKS, INC.
Publishing Division
5810 Ruatan Street
Berwyn Heights, MD 20740

Originally published
Northampton, Mass.:
Press of Gazette Printing Co.
1891

— Publisher's Notice —
In reprints such as this, it is often not possible to remove blemishes from the original. We feel the contents of this book warrant its reissue despite these blemishes and hope you will agree and read it with pleasure.

International Standard Book Number
Paperbound: 978-0-7884-2972-9

PREFACE.

No history of the town having been published since that by Dr. Jacob Porter in 1834, it seemed to me desirable and proper that another should be written. The old records being in my care made it an easy matter to refer to them constantly in compiling this work. It is believed that all dates given can be relied on as accurate, being taken from the original records, with very few exceptions. The history by Dr. Porter has been of great assistance. I have also obtained some facts from the Hampshire County Gazetteer, and also from an article in the "Magazine of American History," of March, 1887, by Mrs. Martha J. Lamb. I am also indebted to Mr. Levi Clark. Mr. Levi N. Campbell, Mr. Chas. Lyman Shaw, and others, for information furnished. The genealogical record of some of the original settlers has been omitted because their descendants have all long since removed or deceased,—and others because their records are very imperfect.

The plates of portrait of Charles Dudley Warner, his birthplace, and the present church and town hall were kindly loaned by Messrs. Wade, Warner & Co., proprietors of "Picturesque Hampshire," for use in this work.

CONTENTS.

CHAPTER I.

SITUATION AND EXTENT.—BOUNDARIES, ANGLES AND MEASUREMENTS.—SURFACE.—STREAMS AND PONDS.—FISH.—MINERALS.—SOIL.—PRODUCTIONS.—TIMBER.

CHAPTER II.

EARLY CIVIL HISTORY.—"HATFIELD EQUIVALENT."—GRANTS.—FIRST SETTLERS.—FIRST TOWN MEETING.—SUBSEQUENT MEETINGS.—LIST OF SELECTMEN.—TOWN CLERKS.—REPRESENTATIVES IN GENERAL COURT.

CHAPTER III.

CHURCH HISTORY.—EARLY MINISTERS.—ORGANIZATION OF FIRST CHURCH.—LIST OF ORIGINAL MEMBERS.—FIRST MEETING-HOUSE.—PRICE OF MATERIALS.—PLAN OF INTERIOR.—DEDICATION.—BELFRY AND BELL.—SUNDRY ITEMS.—CALL AND SETTLEMENT OF REV. MOSES HALLOCK.—INSTALLATION.—ENTERTAINMENT.

CHAPTER IV.

SKETCH OF REV. MOSES HALLOCK.—HIS SCHOOL.—ANECDOTES.—COLLEAGUE CALLED.—REV. DANA GOODSELL.—"STOP THAT PREPARATION."—HIS SUCCESSORS.—DEACONS.—PRESENT MEETING-HOUSE.—DANIELS FUND.—ORGANIZATION OF FIRST PARISH.—BAPTIST SOCIETY,—ADVENT CHAPEL.

CHAPTER V.

SCHOOLS,—FIRST LOCATION OF HOUSES.—NUMBER INCREASED.—REDUCED IN NUMBER AND RE-LOCATED.—"MOVING COMMITTEE."—INCIDENTS OF REMOVING.—DISTRICT SYSTEM.—LIST OF SCHOOL COMMITTEE.—STATISTICS.—NAMES OF PRESENT PUPILS IN THE PUBLIC SCHOOLS.

CHAPTER VI.

TOWN HALL.—ROADS.—EARLY MODES OF TRAVEL.—LOST IN THE WOODS.—EARLY BRIDGE BUILDING.—PRESENT SYSTEM OF REPAIRING ROADS.—ROAD COMMISSIONERS.—NAMES OF STREETS.—POST OFFICES.—POSTMASTERS.—FIRST MAIL SUPPLY.—PRESENT MAIL FACILITIES.—EARLY RATES OF POSTAGE.

CHAPTER VII.

CEMETERIES.—BILL OF MORTALITY.—LIST OF AGED DECEASED,—SUICIDES,—SUDDEN DEATHS.

CHAPTER VIII.

STORES AND MANUFACTURES.—JOHN MACK.—I. K. LINCOLN AND OTHERS.—JACOB AND LEVI CLARK.—LEONARD CAMPBELL.—STORES AT PRESENT TIME.—ROBINSON'S CORN MILL.—WARNER, WHITING & CO.—STREETER'S FACTORY.—TANNERY.—OTHER MANUFACTURES.

CHAPTER IX.

PHYSICIANS.—DR. TORREY.—DR. PORTER.—DR. SAMUEL SHAW.—"HIT HIM ANOTHER."—LATER PRACTITIONERS.—JUSTICES OF THE PEACE.

CHAPTER X.

REVOLUTIONARY PENSIONERS.—SOLDIERS OF 1812.—ARTILLERY COMPANY.—LIST OF SOLDIERS IN WAR OF THE REBELLION.—DEATHS AMONG.—G. A. R. POST.

CHAPTER XI.

COLLEGE GRADUATES AND PROFESSIONAL MEN.

CHAPTER XII.

CENSUS.—VALUATION.—LIST OF VOTERS.—POLITICAL PARTIES.—CAMPAIGN OF 1840. BITS FROM THE OLD RECORDS.—INCIDENTS AND REMINISCENCES.—FIRES.

CHAPTER XIII.

PERSONS NOW LIVING HERE OVER 75.—FOREIGNERS.—OLD HOUSES.—GENERAL TYPE—ORIGINAL DWELLINGS NOW STANDING.—SINGING SCHOOLS.—"THE OLD VILLAGE CHOIR."—DRAMATIC CLUB.—"SADDLE THE DOGS."—CONTRAST.

INDEX OF GENEALOGICAL HISTORY.

EBENEZER BISBEE.
JOSEPH BEALS.
JOHN CAMPBELL.
ABRAM CLARK.
JACOB CLARK.
ANDREW COOK.
JESSE DYER.
JOSEPH GLOYD.
MOSES HALLOCK.
JOHN HAMLEN.
JACOB JONES.

ISAAC JOY.
JACOB NASH.
BARNABAS PACKARD.
JAMES RICHARDS.
JOSIAH SHAW.
SAMUEL STREETER.
JOSIAH TORREY.
AMOS TIRRELL.
EILJAH WARNER.
CALEB WHITE.
DAVID WHITON.

JACOB WHITMARSH.

LIST OF ILLUSTRATIONS.

CHARLES N. DYER.
FIRST MEETING HOUSE.
PLAN OF INTERIOR.
CHURCH AND TOWN HALL.
MILL OF MOUNTAIN MILLER.
DR. SAMUEL SHAW.

CHARLES DUDLEY WARNER.
HIS BIRTHPLACE.
LEVI N. CAMPBELL.
LOUIS L. CAMPBELL.
LEAVITT HALLOCK.
FREEMAN HAMLEN.

CHAPTER I.

SITUATION AND EXTENT.—BOUNDARIES. ANGLES AND MEASUREMENTS.—SURFACE.—
STREAMS AND PONDS.—FISH.—MINERALS.—SOIL.—PRODUCTIONS.—TIMBER.

Plainfield is situated in the extreme north-west corner of Hampshire County, twenty miles north-west from Northampton. It has an area of about twenty square miles, measuring about five miles east and west, and four miles north and south. It is bounded on the north by Hawley, east by Ashfield, both in Franklin Co., south by Cummington, and west by Windsor and Savoy, both in Berkshire Co. According to a survey made by Eliphalet Darling in 1831, by order of the General Court, the boundary lines and angles are as follows: Beginning at the N. W. corner, which is nearly a mile north of Edward W. Mason's, where A. N. Remington formerly lived, thence running E. 19.° S. four miles, 314 rods to the N. E. corner, this line being the boundary between Hawley and Plainfield. The N. E. corner is about 125 rods north of the former residence of L. N. Campbell, where G. W. Billings now lives. From this corner, the boundary between Ashfield and Plainfield runs S. 17° W. 217 rods, thence S. 30' E. 122 rods, thence E. 19° 20' S. 85 rods, thence S. 19° 20' W. 401 rods, thence S. 30' E. 517 rods to the S. E. corner, this being also the S. W. corner of Ashfield. The N. E. corner of Cummington is about three-fourths of a mile east of this corner. The monument marking the S. E. corner of Plainfield, is about three-fourths of a mile N. E. of the house of James W. Loud. The boundary between Cummington and Plainfield runs from this corner, W. 17° S. 195 rods, thence W. 20° N. five miles and four rods to the S. W. corner and Windsor line, running over the summit of Deer Hill. This corner is in a small mow lot not quite half a mile N. W. of the mill of the L. L. Brown Paper Co. in West Cummington. The boundary between Windsor and Plainfield runs from this corner N. 18° W. two miles and 287 rods to a monument which marks the N. E. corner of Windsor. This is about fifty rods S. of Geo. A. Blanchard's. Thence running W. 18° N. 166 rods to Savoy line. This corner is about sixty rods S. of Edward W. Mason's, and not far from the South Pond in Windsor. The line between Savoy and Plainfield runs from this corner N. 18° E. one mile to the place of beginning. These lines are perambulated and the marks and bounds renewed whenever necessary by the Selectmen of Plainfield in company with the Selectmen of the adjoining town, once in five years, according to law. The Ashfield line was last run Nov. 15, 1886—Cummington and Windsor in Oct. 1888—Savoy, Nov. 6, 1890—Hawley, Nov. 17, 1890. Plainfield was incorporated later than any of the adjoining towns. The geographical center is near the house of Wm. C. Whiting.

SURFACE.

This township lies on the eastern side of the Green Mountains. It is divided into two nearly equal portions by Mill Brook, the largest stream in town, which rising near Hawley line, flows S. W. and S. and empties into the north branch of the Westfield in Cummington, a few rods east of the "Otis" bridge. Two ranges of hills traverse the town from north to south on each side of Mill brook, the highest points of these ranges being about equi-distant from the brook and the eastern and western boundaries of the town. The west range is considerably higher than the east, the highest points being named as follows, beginning at the north. The heights given are from the late official survey. Beals Hill, 1980 feet high, the summit of which is just across the line in Hawley, derived its name from the fact that Samuel Beals, one of the early settlers lived on it, well up toward the summit, as well as his son Dennis, who spent his life on the same spot. This house we believe is still standing; the town line runs through it. The Beals however always claimed their residence and voted in Plainfield. South of this is Bond Hill, the origin of the name being unknown. Then West Mountain, 2160 ft.—the highest point in Western Hampshire. Further south is Deer Hill, 2020 feet high, so called, tradition says, because large numbers of deer made it their headquarters in the earlier times. Magnificent views are to be obtained from their summits, particularly from West and Deer Hills, and our summer residents never fail to visit one or more of them for that purpose. Standing on these hills, one may see Haystack Mt. in Vt. on the north, Monadnock in N. H. in the north-east, Mt. Lincoln in Pelham on the east, Chester and Blandford on the south, Saddle Mt. in the north-west and Hoosac Mt., under which passes the famous Hoosac Tunnel. With a good field-glass one may discover many other points of interest. The east range is much broader than the west, forming a gently undulating table land, which decreases in breadth toward the south part, and ends abruptly near the Cummington line. The only abrupt elevation on this range, and even this slopes gently south and east, is at the north end of the range. It is proposed to name this elevation, which is 1900 feet high, Mt. Warner, in honor of Charles Dudley Warner, who was born and reared on its heights. From this east range the town undoubtedly derives its name. It is nearly two miles in breadth at the widest part, and falls toward the south at the rate of about 100 feet to the mile. The village is built near the top and on the western slope. The house of the late Dea. Freeman Hamlen, in the upper part of the village, is just 1700 feet above sea level.

STREAMS AND PONDS.

The principal streams besides Mill Brook, are Meadow brook and "the Grant" brook. The former is made by the union of three small streams which take their rise on the old Ebenezer Nash farm, a short distance east of Russell Tirrell's, and flowing south-east passing near Wm. H. Dyer's and No. 2 school-house, finally empties into the Westfield at Cummington Village. The Grant brook, so called because it passes through the tract of land known as Wainwright's grant, of which we shall speak later, takes its rise on the 'Squire Clark place, now occupied by A. L. Richmond, and flowing south-east through "the Hollow" near David Packard's and Samuel Parker's, enters a corner of Ashfield, thence to Cummington, where it becomes the north branch of Swift River, emptying into the Westfield at Swift River P. O. The town abounds in durable springs and nearly all dwelling-houses, and also barns, are supplied from them

STREAMS AND PONDS.

with running water. The upper village is supplied by an aqueduct from a never failing spring, half a mile north; the lower village from several springs. Wooden pipes made from spruce trees five or six inches in diameter, are in many instances used for an aqueduct. When laid in wet or moist ground, they often last until worn through by the action of the water.

There are two natural ponds, the North and Crooked, both in the north-west part of the town. The North pond is about a mile long and half a mile in width in the widest part. The outlet is in a northerly direction and empties into the Deerfield river above Charlemont, while the waters of the Crooked pond, which takes its name from its form, flow south-westerly into the South pond in Windsor, which is the head of one of the branches of the Westfield river. Both the first named ponds are on high land and the outlet streams fall very rapidly. The Crooked pond though only three-fourths of a mile from the South pond, is probably 200 feet higher. The North pond is a much handsomer body of water than the Crooked, the shores for the most part being hard and gravelly, while those of the Crooked are muddy, the waters being shallow and dotted with stumps, Both have been raised somewhat by dams. These ponds contain pickerel and perch. The pickerel increase but slowly, from the fact that it devours nearly all of its young. It is a sort of fresh water shark, feeding on almost any fish smaller than itself. One specimen caught on being opened was found to contain another recently swallowed, and this contained a third one. The writer believes that stocking these ponds with pickerel was a great mistake. The North pond was the natural home of the trout, and if the pickerel had not been introduced, it might now under the protection of the fish and game laws, have been well filled with this most desirable fish. Perch were introduced into these ponds about twenty years since, and have now become plentiful. Nature has furnished them with weapons which enable them to successfully defend themselves and their young from the attacks of the pickerel. They are easily taken with hook and line, while the pickerel are only caught by the expert angler, and but seldom by him. The most successful mode of capturing the pickerel is practiced in winter, hooks being set in holes cut through the ice. This method, however, if the ice be thick is attended with considerable labor. It is hoped that some time in the future they may be wholly exterminated from these ponds. The various streams are moderately well stocked with trout, and if they were absolutely protected throughout the year for four or five years they would attain considerable size and numbers.

MINERALS AND SOIL.

Dr. Porter, in his history of the town published in 1834, gives a full treatise on its geology and mineralogy. As the writer is neither a geologist or mineralogist, these subjects will be omitted in this work. Any one who wishes information on these topics, I would respectfully refer to "Porter's History of Plainfield," several copies of which are still preserved in town and elsewhere. I will only say that with one exception no valuable minerals have been discovered here, at least not in sufficient quantities to be of any commercial value. The exception referred to is manganese or oxide of manganese. This is found in the southwest part of the town, on the farm of Wm. H. Packard, and also on Allen Thayer's. It was mined to some extent on the Packard farm years ago, and it is understood that it was found in paying quantities, but for some reason the enterprise was abandoned. Outside parties have recently leased a portion of the farm for this purpose, and will soon commence operations. Iron ore, said to be of superior quality, has been dug on the old Robinson place, now owned by Allen Thayer, about one and one-half miles west of the village, but has not yet been developed in paying quantities. Some years since gold was discovered on West Hill, in the dirt thrown out by a woodchuck in digging his hole. It was afterward ascertained, however, that the "claim" had been "salted" with small specimens of genuine California ore, by a young man living in the vicinity, who wished to create a little excitement. The soil is a heavy loam, varying in different localities. It has become somewhat exhausted, and produces good crops only by the use of fertilizers, which in early times were not considered essential. Much flax was then raised without fertilizers, the same piece of ground being sown for several years in succession in many instances. Flax being a very exhausting crop, much of the land on which it was raised has never recovered its fertility.

PRODUCTIONS AND TIMBER.

Corn, oats, barley, rye and buckwheat are successfully raised, as well as all kinds of garden vegetables, with the exception of onions and melons. Potatoes are so liable to be affected by rot that they are now considered a very uncertain crop. Fifty or sixty years ago the price of corn was one dollar per bushel, varying but little from that price. Nearly all the corn was raised at home, very little if any being brought into town. It was nearly all used for food, it being almost an unheard of thing to feed corn or Indian meal to neat stock or horses. A little was fed to swine. Considerable quantities of corn are now sown, which is used green as feed for milch cows, or cured for winter use. It is also used as ensilage to a limited extent, a few of the farmers having built silos for that purpose. By using fertilizers, many tons of this can be produced on an acre, and it is considered a profitable crop. The western or "horse tooth" variety is generally sown for this purpose, though sweet corn is sometimes used. The exhausted condition of our pastures makes it necessary for farmers to produce some green crop to be used after the month of August as feed for milch cows. As yet no fertilizers are applied to pastures, being used only on field and garden crops, and as top-dressing for meadows. The native trees are principally maple, beech, birch, cherry, ash, hemlock and spruce. Elm, bass, poplar, pine and balsam are occasionally met with, but are not as common as the first named. Each of the first five are found in two or more distinct varieties. Oak, chestnut and hickory do not grow in the limits of the town. The writer is informed by an old resident, that so far as known, only one chestnut tree has ever arrived at maturity here. This stood about half a mile north of the meeting-house, but was struck by lightning and destroyed many years since. Very little of the original growth of timber is now standing, though first growth rock maples are still quite common, and a few beeches yet remain. Scarcely any first quality spruce lumber is now produced in town. Enough second quality may be had for such dimension lumber and rough boarding as are needed by the inhabitants for building purposes. Finishing lumber, clapboards and shingles are mostly obtained from lumber dealers in the larger towns. Clapboards from native bass are occasionally used. Hard wood lands when cleared without burning, are soon covered with a growth of spruce and hemlock, while soft wood lands cleared in the same way, are apt to spring up to cherry, white birch or poplar. The price for hard body wood is $3 per cord, delivered. One of the first things attended to by the early settlers after being comfortably located, was the setting out of an apple orchard. These in most cases flourished and bore fruit well. Many of these produced only natural fruit, a part only being grafted. From the natural fruit great quantities of cider were manufactured, every farmer putting into the cellar for use during the year at least six or eight barrels, and many a much larger quantity. Some of these ancient apple trees still remain and the site of some of the old houses is marked by the proximity of a few of these trees. Other orchards have taken their places, and the town now produces of grafted fruit in an average year, more than double enough for the use of the inhabitants. On account of the elevated situation, grapes and peaches do not thrive. Pears do rather better. Blackberries grow wild in abundance. Raspberries and wild strawberries are less plenty.

CHAPTER II.

EARLY CIVIL HISTORY.—"HATFIELD EQUIVALENT."—GRANTS.—FIRST SETTLERS.—
FIRST TOWN MEETING.—SUBSEQUENT MEETINGS.—LIST OF SELECTMEN.—TOWN
CLERKS.—REPRESENTATIVES IN GENERAL COURT.

Plantation No. 5, which included both Cummington and Plainfield, was sold at public vendue, June 2, 1762, at the "Royal Exchange Tavern in King St.," Boston, to John Cummings, for 1800 pounds, he paying twenty pounds down and giving a bond for the remainder. At a division of lots, Dec. 29, 1762, the names of twenty-seven others are recorded as having become proprietors. March 16, 1785, the north part of Cummington was set off and incorporated as the District of Plainfield. It appears that the state for some public service performed had given a certain tract of land to the town of Hatfield. This land was afterwards incorporated into the area of other towns, and a section north and west was given to Hatfield in its stead. This latter was known as "Hatfield Equivalent." Plantation No. 5, when surveyed, was found to include a large part of this "Equivalent." What the exact limits of this tract were I am unable to ascertain. It was probably as large as an ordinary township, and extended north into the east part of Hawley, beyond the southwest corner of Buckland and possibly to Charlemont. In shape it was irregular, the south part extending further west than the north part. Frequent mention is made of the tract in the early town records and deeds. It is certain that it extended south within half a mile at least of Cummington line. The farm of John Hamlen, now occupied by E. A. Atkins, the farm of Marshall Stetson, and also that of Ebenezer Nash, lying east of Russell Tirrell's, are described in the several deeds as consisting of certain lots, designated by number, of Hatfield Equivalent. Simon Burroughs, who lived just north of J. W. Sears, is mentioned as being a resident of Hatfield Equivalent. "At a Legal Meeting of the Inhabitants of the District of Plainfield, at Samuel Streetor's barn, on the twenty Ninth Day of July, A. D. 1788, Voted that they would take no Notice of the Request of No. 7 (Hawley) which was as Follows, Viz.: first that they had Enominated Nine men, and we Should choose one out of Sd Number, and the Equivalent one and No. 7 the third, to Settle the dispute respecting the Equivalent being annexed to Plainfield, if not they would leave it to the Selectmen of three Towns which they Enominated, and if we would not comply with either of the proposals they would have us make them some," &c. March 16, 1789, "Voted that Capt. John Cunningham, Jeremiah Robinson and Simon Burroughs [serve] as a Committee to meet the Committees from No. 7, Charlemont and Hatfield Equivalent, in order to Choose an Indifferant Committee to Determine the Dispute that has so long Subsisted between No. 7, Plainfield, and Hatfield Equivalent." Several similar votes were passed during the next year or two, and the matter appears to have been settled before 1794, for the record of a meeting held April 7, 1794, states that " made choice of Peter B. Beals, as a Committee to Examine into the matter concerning the Vacancyes laid out in what was formally called Hatfield Equivalent," &c. March 12, 1792, "Voted to accept of a Tract of Land lying east of Plainfield and west of Ashfield, with the Inhabitants living thereon." The only inhabitants living on this tract, so far as known, were Joseph Clark and Jonathan Beals, and their families. This tract was a gore not previously included in the limits of any town, and was bounded as follows: Beginning at a point on the present Ashfield line nearly due east from Wm. Jones's, thence following said line to the southwest corner of Ashfield, thence west 17° south 195 rods on the present Cummington line, thence a little east of north in a direct line to the place of beginning. This last described line crossed the road which leads by Geo. E. Harris's, passing very near where his house now stands. Joseph Clark, before named, lived in a house which stood a few rods east of Harris's. Jonathan Beals, it is supposed, lived about one-fourth of a mile south, on an old road, now discontinued. June 21, 1803, one mile of the south side of Hawley was set off to the District of Plainfield, since which time the town lines have remained unaltered. May 15, 1806, it was "voted unanimously to petition the General Court to set off the District of Plainfield from Cummington and incorporate it into a town." This was accordingly done June 15, 1807. So far as appears, districts had all the privileges of towns, except that they had no representative in General Court and were joined to some other town for the purpose of obtaining such representation.

"THE GRANT."

A tract in the northeast part of the town was early granted to Mr. Mayhew for services among the Indians.

EARLY SETTLERS.

The north part of this grant was soon after transferred to one Wainwright, whose name it subsequently bore. The boundaries of Wainwright's grant are believed to be as follows: Beginning at the northwest corner, the same being the northeast corner of the Ebenezer Nash farm, thence running easterly on the south line of the farm now owned by A. L. Richmond, and continuing on the same range to Ashfield line; this was the northern boundary. The western boundary ran from the first named corner southerly on the east line of the Ebenezer Nash farm, Stephen Parsons's and H. S. Packard's lands to the northeast corner of the Rufus P. Bates lot, now owned by Homer Cook. The south line ran easterly from this corner to Ashfield line, following the range of the north line of the Bates lot. This grant contained about 1000 acres.

EARLY SETTLERS.

Most of the early settlers came from Abington, Bridgewater and Weymouth, Mass. The first settler who resided within the present limits of the town was a Scotchman named McIntire, who came here with his family in 1770, and located near where Mrs. Mary A. Dunning now lives, in the north part of the town. The following persons, and doubtless a number of others, had settled here before 1780, viz. : Lieut. Joshua Shaw, Andrew Cook, Isaac Joy, Caleb White, Lieut. Ebenezer Colson, Lieut. Samuel Noyes, Ebenezer Bisbee, Abram Beals, John Streeter, Jonathan Monroe, and Noah Packard. The first birth recorded is that of Hannah Cook, Oct. 6, 1774, daughter of Andrew Cook.

FIRST TOWN MEETING.

The following is a copy of the warrant calling the first town meeting, and also of the record of the proceedings at that meeting :

HAMPSHIRE, ss. To Isaac Joy of Plainfield, in the County of Hampshire, aforesaid, yeoman, Greeting: Pursuant to an act of the Commonwealth for erecting the Northerly part of Cummington, in the County of Hampshire, into a District by the Name of Plainfield, and investing the Inhabitants of the said District with all the Privileges and Immunities that other Towns or Districts within this Commonwealth Do Enjoy; Also Impowering Nahum Eager, Esqr. to Issue his Warrant Directed to Some Principle Inhabitant of sd District, Requiring him to call a meeting of said Inhabitants in order to Choose Town Officers, as by Law Towns or Districts are Impowered to Choose in the month of March Annually; These are therefore in the Name of the Commonwealth of Massachusetts to Require you the sd Isaac Joy to Notify and Warn the Inhabitants of the sd District of Plainfield, that they assemble themselves together at the Dwelling-house of Mr. Simon Burroughs, in said Plainfield, on Monday, the 25th Day of July, Instant, at One of the Clock in the afternoon, then and there to Choose all such Officers as Towns within this Commonwealth are Impowered to Choose in the month of March Annually. Hereof you nor they may not fail. Given under my Hand and Seal at Worthington, this 14th Day of July, A. D. 1785. NAHUM EAGER, Justice Peace.

" At a legal meeting of the Inhabitants of the District of Plainfield, at the dwelling-house of Mr. Simon Burroughs, in said district, on Monday, the 25th day of July, A. D., 1785, Lieut. Ebenezer Colson was chosen Moderator; Lieut. Joshua Shaw, District Clerk; Lieut. Ebenezer Colson, Lieut. John Packard and Lieut. John Cunningham, Selectmen; Lieut. Joshua Shaw, District Treasurer; Simon Burroughs, Constable; Isaac Joy and Lieut. John Packard, Tythingmen; Josiah Torrey, Solomon Nash, Nathan Fay, William Daniels, Jacob Clark, Abijah Pool, Jonathan Munroe, David White and Daniel Streetor, Surveyors of Highways; Lieut. Samuel Noyes, Surveyor of Lumber; Daniel Streetor, Sealer of Leather; John Streetor, Fence Viewer; Asa Joy and Azariah Beals, Hogreeves; David White, Field Driver; John Streetor, Deer-rieff; the meeting dissolved." Simon Burroughs, at whose house this meeting was held, lived about twelve rods north of J. W. Sears's house (formerly occupied by Newell Dyer.) The site of the Burroughs house can still be distinctly traced. It was torn down one night by some citizens to prevent its occupancy by a negro family who were about to move into it. The next eight meetings were held "at the dwelling-house of Mr. Jonathan Munroe," whose house stood where that of the late Lewis Shaw now stands; then at "Capt. John Cunningham's new barn." This was on what is now known as the "Strong place," about a mile north of the village. During the summer and winter of 1788, town meetings, which were frequent in those days, were held at Samuel Streetor's barn. Then a meeting "to choose one Governor, one Lt. Governor, and four Senators," was held April 6, 1789, in "Capt. Cunningham's new barn;" again, May 11, 1789, a meeting "to vote for a Representative for the Great and General Court" (with Cummington) was held at Lieut. David White's. By this time the voters had evidently had enough of "barn" meetings, and until August, 1792, meetings were held "at the dwelling-house of Mr. Samuel Streetor." This house stood where S. H. Sears's house now stands, just north of the meeting-house, or possibly it might have been the present structure, which was erected about that time. Aug. 20, 1792, the first meeting-house was sufficiently completed for a town-meeting to be held in it, and it was ever afterwards used for such meetings, as well as for service on the Sabbath. Only those persons having a freehold estate of the annual income of three pounds, or any other estate to the value of sixty pounds, were allowed to vote for State officers.

LIST OF SELECTMEN.

The following is a list of Selectmen from 1785 to the present time (1891,) with the year of their first election, and number of years service:

	First Elected.	Years of Service.
Ebenezer Colson,	1785	3
John Packard,	"	3
John Cunningham,	"	11
Caleb White,	1786	4
David White,	"	1
Isaac Joy,	1788	2
Ebenezer Bisbee,	"	15
James Porter,	"	1
James Richards,	1790	21
Jeremiah Robinson,	1791	1
Joseph Beals,	1795	1
Thomas Shaw,	1798	3
James Hayward,	"	2
Ebenezer Colson, Jr.,	1799	7
John Hamlen,	1800	19
Peter B. Beals,	1803	1
Amos Crittenden,	1804	1
Elijah Warner,	"	18
Nehemiah Joy,	1808	2
Jacob Joy,	1814	1
Robert Beals,	1819	4

LIST OF SELECTMEN.

	First Elected.	Years of Service.
Iram Packard,	1821	4
John Packard, Jr.,	1822	5
John Mack,	1824	3
Justus Warner,	1825	2
Samuel Shaw,	1826	8
Erastus Bates,	1828	3
Jacob Pratt,	1831	3
Isaac K. Lincoln,	1832	2
John Carr,	1833	3
Samuel White,	1834	4
Stephen Gloyd,	1835	12
William Robinson,	1836	4
Jerijah Barber,	1837	7
Albert Dyer,	1840	4
Wm. N. Ford,	1842	4
Elias Giddings,	1843	1
Stephen Hayward,	1845	6
Freeman Hamlen,	1846	6
Wm. A. Hawley,	1848	2
Levi N. Campbell,	1849	22
Wanton C. Gilbert,	1854	1
Lewis Shaw,	"	18
Samuel W. Lincoln,	1855	8
Samuel Dyer,	"	1
Joseph Sears,	1857	6
Fordyce Whitmarsh,	1858	2
Merritt Torrey,	1860	7
Merritt Jones,	1863	1
Jacob W. Pratt,	1867	5
Homer Cook,	1871	11
Stephen Hayward, Jr.,	1872	2

	First Elected.	Years of Service.
Seth W. Clark,	1873	6
James A. Nash,	1874	9
James A. Winslow,	1876	2
Edwin A. Atkins,	1878	2
Levi W. Gloyd,	1883	5
Joseph W. Sears,	1887	1
Albert N. Gurney,	1888	3
Harold S. Packard,	"	2
Daniel H. Gould,	1890	1

The present board elected March 2, 1891, are—Albert N. Gurney, Daniel H. Gould, Joseph W. Sears. The Selectmen have always served as Assessors and Overseers of the Poor.

LIST OF TOWN CLERKS.

The following is a list of Town Clerks since 1785, with the year of their first election and number of years service. Town Clerks have, without exception, been chosen and served as Town Treasurer:

	First Elected.	Years of Service.
Joshua Shaw,	1785	10
John Cunningham,	1795	2
James Richards,	1797	4
Thomas Shaw,	1801	14
John Mack,	1815	3
Cyrus Joy,	1818	3
Robert Beals,	1821	7
Justus Warner,	1828	1
Leavitt Hallock,	1829	2
Erastus Bates,	1831	1

REPRESENTATIVES IN GENERAL COURT.

	First Elected.	Years of Service.
John Mack, Jr.,	1832	1
Jason Richards,	1833	12
Jacob Clark,	1841	3
Levi Clark,	1848	5
Freeman Hamlen,	1853	23
Charles N. Dyer,	1876	15

REPRESENTATIVES IN GENERAL COURT.

Since the incorporation of Plainfield as a town in 1808, the following persons have had the honor of representing the town in the Legislature. When no dates are given the town was not represented:

1808–9–10,	John Cunningham.
1811–12,	James Richards.
1813–14–15,	John Hamlen.
1816,	James Richards.
1819,	Cyrus Joy.
1821,	Elijah Warner.
1823–26,	John Hamlen.
1827,	Elijah Warner.
1828–29–30,	John Mack.
1831–2–3–4,	Erastus Bates.
1835–36,	Elijah Clark.
1837,	John Carr.
1839–40,	Stephen Gloyd.
1841–42,	Jason Richards.
1844–46,	Jerijah Barber.
1849,	Leavitt Hallock.
1850–51,	Freeman Hamlen.
1852-53,	Wanton C. Gilbert.
1854,	Levi N. Campbell.

Mr. Campbell was the last elected under the old system. The present district system went into operation in 1857, and the following named were elected from Plainfield to serve in the years named:

1860,	Samuel W. Lincoln.
1864,	Levi N. Campbell.
1871,	Stephen Hayward, Jr.
1877,	Merritt Torrey.
1884,	James A. Winslow.
1891,	Edwin A. Atkins.

The district at first comprised the towns of Cummington, Goshen, Middlefield, Plainfield and Worthington. In 1866 Chesterfield was added, in 1876 Huntington, and in 1886 Westhampton.

CHAPTER III.

CHURCH HISTORY.—EARLY MINISTERS.—ORGANIZATION OF FIRST CHURCH.—LIST OF ORIGINAL MEMBERS.—FIRST MEETING-HOUSE.—PRICE OF MATERIALS.—PLAN OF INTERIOR.—DEDICATION.—BELFRY AND BELL.—SUNDRY ITEMS.—CALL AND SETTLEMENT OF REV. MOSES HALLOCK.—INSTALLATION.—ENTERTAINMENT.

Previous to the incorporation of Plainfield as a district, the inhabitants attended church at Cummington, and formed part of the ministerial charge of the Rev. James Briggs. One of the first acts of the settlers after being set off from Cummington, was to take measures to provide stated preaching. Aug. 11, 1785, "Voted to raise 14 pound to hire preaching the present year," also, "Voted that Isaac Joy, Lieut. John Packard and Lieut. John Cunningham be a committee to hire a Gospel Minister to preach with us." Sept. 5, 1785, "Voted that the west side the brook inhabitants should have their proportionable part of the preaching on that side said brook," July 24, 1786, "Voted to agree with Mr. James Thompson to preach with us four Sabbaths on probation." May 14, 1787, "Voted unanimously to give Mr. James Thompson a call to settle in the work of the ministry among us." This for some reason was not accepted. It seems that Mr. Thompson was not the first who preached here, for March 12, 1787: "Voted to allow Andrew Cook's account for boarding Mr. Hatch while he was preaching with us, 19s, and what he paid Mr. Hatch for preaching, 6 pounds."

HISTORY OF PLAINFIELD.

ORGANIZATION OF FIRST CHURCH.

Plainfield, Aug. 31, 1786. At the desire of a number of the inhabitants of Plainfield, a district of Cummington, convened the Rev. Timothy Allen, James Briggs and Elisha Fish, to lead them in forming into a church state. The Rev. Timothy Allen was chosen Moderator, and Elisha Fish, Scribe. Mr. James Thompson, preacher of the gospel, was invited to sit and assist in this business. Accordingly the aforesaid inhabitants of Plainfield presented themselves and exhibited such satisfactory evidence by letters from the churches to which they belonged, and by answering to questions propounded to them, of the propriety of proceeding to incorporate them into a church state, that the Rev'd gentlemen aforesaid thought fit, and accordingly did incorporate said persons into a visible church of Christ.

TIMOTHY ALLEN, *Moderator.*
Attest,
ELISHA FISH, *Scribe.*

This is a true copy of the proceedings of the council who formed the persons aforesaid into a visible church of Christ in Plainfield.
Attest,
MOSES HALLOCK, now pastor of said church.

The following is a list of the original members:

Andrew Ford,	Martha Nash,
Sarah Ford,	Elijah Ford,
John Packard,	Solomon Ford,
Hannah Packard,	Amy White,
Andrew Ford, Jr.,	Martha Town,
Sarah Ford,	Martha Robinson,
Solomon Nash,	Molly Packard.

This church celebrated the 100th anniversary of its incorporation, Aug. 31, 1886. An address of welcome was given by the acting pastor, Rev. F. G. Webster, and Rev. Solomon Clark, a former pastor, delivered a most interesting discourse. Homan Hallock, son of Rev. Moses, Rev. Leavitt H. Hallock of Portland, Me., Rev. Wm. Hallock of New Jersey, and Charles Hallock, grandson of the same, were present and made short addresses, and in other ways added greatly to the interest of the occasion. The exercises occupied nearly the whole day, many former residents being present and taking part in the exercises. The church now has 78 resident members, and 12 non-resident.

FIRST MEETING HOUSE—LOOKING NORTHWEST.

Aug. 16, 1787, a committee was appointed "to measure and find the center of Plainfield, and likewise to agree upon a place which they shall think most proper for erecting a meeting-house upon." May 23, 1791, "Voted that the spot of ground west of the road leading from Samuel Streetor's to Robinson's corn-mill, and south of the road leading from Samuel Streetor's to his saw-mill, and joining upon said roads, be the spot of ground to build a meeting-house upon; 67 yeas and 4 nays." Oct. 27, 1791, it was voted to build the meeting-house on the spot fixed upon, and that the dimensions should be 55½x42½. Nov. 3, "Voted that Caleb White, Capt. John Cunningham, Capt. James Richards, Andrew Cook, and John Hamlen be a committee to receive notes of those persons who purchase Pews, likewise that they procure material and carry on the building said meeting-house in such a manner as shall be most advantageous to the district." The following prices were established for materials, delivered on the spot:

Good Hemlock boards, £1-6s. per M.
" Spruce " 1-6 "
" " Clapboards, 1-6 "
" Ash Slitwork, 3-4, 1-10 "
" Pine boards, inch thick, 3-0 "

Nails were estimated by count instead of by the lb. 10d nails, 9s. per M.; 8d nails, 6s. 8d. per M.; 4d nails, 3s. per M. Voted that the joints in the roof before shingling be covered with birch bark. April 23, 1792, "Voted that the owners of pews in the meeting-house provide rum to raise said building." The meeting-house was raised soon after, but owing to the limited resources of the district it was not completed until 1797, five years afterwards. It was dedicated June 15, 1797. Two sermons were preached on the occasion, one by Rev. Aaron Bascom of Chester, and the other by Rev. John Leland of Partridgefield, (now Peru.) The meeting-house contained 44 pews below and 19 in the gallery, ranged on the outside against the wall. The gallery was on three sides, the singers' seats being in front of the gallery pews. Two were afterwards added below and two above. The plan of the interior was copied from the town records. The original was the work of Joshua Shaw and James Richards. The figures in each

A hand-drawn seating chart/floor plan (rotated). Reading the pews as labeled:

Top row (left to right): Caleb Beals 22 | John Hamlin 33 | Dr. Solm Bond 19 | Simon Burrvgis 42 | Pulpit | Bertha Hallock | Samuel Streeter 40 | Solomon Pratt 35 | [col...]

Left side (top to bottom): Samuel Seabord 25 | James Nichoras 21 | ...

Right side (top to bottom): Seth Ford 24 | Ebenezer Colson 24 | Joseph Beals 22

Center pews (upper block):
| Luther Packard 35 | Asa Streeter 32 |
| Capt Joh Cunghton | Noah Packard 29 |

Center pews (lower block):
| Jeremiah Robinson 43 | Joseph and Isaac Joy Jr 24 | Asa Joy 28 | John Campbell 23 |
| | Caleb Joy 37 | Benj Town 17 | |

Left center pews:
Azariah Reed 26		
Joseph Mason 21	Solomon Nash 31	Isaac Joy 43
Stephna Smith 21	Barnabas Packard	Jonathan Shaw 41	Jacob Clara 26
John Shaw 22	Ensign Akijah Pool		

Bottom row (left to right): Lt John Packard 24 | Andrew Cook 37 | Elijah Nash 31 | South Doors | Joshua Shaw 39 | Lt Saml Elara 37 | Caleb White 24 | Joseph Beals 22 pew indicate the number of dollars originally paid for it. Above the high pulpit was hung the old-fashioned sounding board, considered an indispensable feature in those days. March 7, 1796, "Voted that the district provide three wands for the tythingmen." A belfry with a steeple was erected in 1800, a bell being procured at the same time. It was cast at New Haven, Ct., by Fenton & Cochrane, and weighs 650 lbs. It is the same bell now in use. Its key was D, but is now nearly D flat, the pitch of instruments having been raised nearly half a tone since the date of its manufacture. There was no means of heating the meeting-house until 1822, when two stoves were procured and placed near the pulpit, not however without considerable opposition. Before this time at the noon intermission during cold weather the people visited Samuel Streetor's and one or two other houses near by to eat the lunch they had brought with them, and absorb heat enough if possible to last them through the long sermon in the afternoon. Most of the elderly ladies carried "foot stoves," in which they placed a dish of glowing coals raked out of "Uncle Sam's" fire place, and carried with them back to meeting. The men meanwhile had taken a little good old rum internally to prevent the cold from piercing their vitals. It was customary for the congregation to stand during the "long prayer." The seats in the pews were hinged and movable. When the occupants of a pew arose, these seats, which ran quite around the pew except the doorway, were lifted, in order to give them more standing room. When the "Amen" was pronounced these seats all came down into place with a bang and clatter which would be astonishing to the present generation. In March, 1791, the church and district voted to

INSTALLATION—ENTERTAINMENT.

give Rev. Moses Hallock a call to settle with them in the work of the gospel ministry. "Voted that the following offers should be made to Mr. Hallock for his settlement and maintenance, viz: Ninety pounds for his settlement and forty-five pounds a year for the first two years, then to increase five pounds a year until it amounts to sixty pounds, there to remain. Mr. Hallock declined the call at this time on account of ill health. March 8, 1792, this call was renewed with the same offers as before, "his settlement and salary to be paid, one quarter in cash, and three quarters in farm produce at cash prices." The following are the prices named for produce:

Rye at 3s. 4d. per bush. Indian Corn at 2s. 8d. per bush.
Grown, grass-fed beef, at 20s. per hundred.
9-score pork at 3½d. per lb.
Good, well dressed flax, at 7d. per lb.

This call being accepted, he was ordained and installed July 11, 1792. The sermon was preached by Rev. Samuel Whitman of Goshen, the text being from Ezekiel 44-23: "And they shall teach my people the difference between the holy and the profane, and cause them to discern between the unclean and the clean." June 14, 1792, "Voted that an invitation be given to Ministers of the Gospel, Candidates for the Ministry, Students of Colleges, together with the Parents, Brethren and Sisters of Mr. Moses Hallock, and such others as he shall see fit to invite, to an Entertainment with the Council, at such place as shall hereafter be appointed. Voted that Capt. John Cunningham make the above Entertainment, in a decent and handsome manner, and lay his account before the district for allowance." Aug. 20, "Voted to allow Capt. John Cunningham ten shillings and three pence for Entertaining the Council at the Ordination of Mr. Moses Hallock."

CHAPTER IV.

SKETCH OF REV. MOSES HALLOCK.—HIS SCHOOL.—ANECDOTES.—COLLEAGUE CALLED. —REV. DANA GOODSELL.—"STOP THAT PREPARATION."—HIS SUCCESSORS.—DEACONS.—PRESENT MEETING-HOUSE.—DANIELS FUND.—ORGANIZATION OF FIRST PARISH.—BAPTIST SOCIETY.—ADVENT CHAPEL.

Rev. Moses Hallock was born on Long Island, Feb. 16, 1760. Before devoting himself to study, he served some time in the Revolutionary army. Graduated at Yale in 1788. His divinity studies were pursued under the instruction of Rev. Samuel Whitman of Goshen, Mass., where his parents resided. The house which he built and in which he lived and died, is now occupied by James Spearman. Except as it has gradually fallen into decay, it remains in nearly the same form in which he left it. It is hoped that in the near future it may be repaired and preserved, on account of the many hallowed associations which cluster around it. His labors during the long period of his ministry were acceptable and useful in a remarkable degree and were greatly blessed. He was respected and beloved by all. Mr. Hallock for thirty years taught a private school, in which he fitted young men for college, they boarding in his house. More than 300 availed themselves of the privileges of this school. Among them were Wm. Cullen Bryant, the poet, James Richards, Jonas King, Pliny Fisk, Levi Parsons and William Richards, foreign missionaries, Dr. Samuel Shaw and Prof. James Hayward. At that time families were more economical and lived on much coarser and plainer food than now. Pies, cakes and sweetmeats as every day articles of food were not used. One gentleman who brought his son to Mr. Hallock to be schooled, told him that at home the boy had been in the habit of having gingerbread, and wished that it might be furnished him at Mr. Hallock's. "Yes," said Mr. Hallock, "he shall have gingerbread." Soon after he said to Mrs. Hallock, in his dry way, "When you make your next batch of brown bread will you please put some *ginger* in it." In illustration of his simple honesty it is related, that owning a farm, he had at one time a pair of young oxen which he wished to sell. One of his neighbors learning the fact, called, and after looking the cattle over said, "I will give you sixty dollars for them." Said Mr. Hallock, "They are not worth so much; you shall have them for *fifty* dollars." In the spring of 1829, after having discharged the duties of his office with uncommon fidelity for nearly thirty-seven years, he made the following communication to his beloved people:

"*To the Inhabitants of the Town of Plainfield:—My Brethren and Friends:* The time approaches when I shall no longer be your minister. This awfully responsible, though pleasant work, must soon be committed to the hands of some other man. I have entered my seventieth year 'and know not the day of my death.' When a parent is about to die he endeavors to set his house in order, that it may be well with his family after his decease. With equal ardor I desire that you as a religious community, may have a good minister of Jesus Christ when my lips shall be unable to teach knowledge. Before I die, I wish to see my pulpit occupied by such a minister; and may he be far more useful to old and young than his predecessor, and as much respected. As soon as you are ready to settle another minister, which will probably be in a year or two, I will consent, the church and congregation requesting it, that the ordaining council should dismiss me

HISTORY OF PLAINFIELD.

on the day of the ordination. It is not uncommon in cases like this, that the town make some provision for the support of the worn out pastor. If you should please by legal vote, to commit to my disposal as my own property, the pew which my family occupy, or some other as valuable, and also to exempt me and the little property I may possess from all kinds of taxation during my life, it will be thankfully accepted." (Signed) MOSES HALLOCK.

Rev. David Kimball was installed colleague pastor with Rev. Mr. Hallock, March 2, 1831. Mr. Hallock died at his home in Plainfield, July 17, 1837, aged 77 years. He was interred in the cemetery north of the church. His tombstone bears the following inscription:

> The Reverend Moses Hallock.
> Born at Brookhaven, L. I., Feb. 16, 1760.
> Reared by Godly parents, Goshen, Mass.
> Graduated at Yale College, 1788.
> Ordained and installed first pastor of the
> Church in Plainfield, July 11, 1792.
> Ministered to a confiding and united people
> 45 years.
> Died July 17, 1837, aged 77 years.
> At 70 he requested a colleague, having
> Received to the church 358 members,
> Instructed 304 pupils—50 became ministers,
> 7 missionaries.
> A man of patriarchal simplicity, integrity,
> Sincerity, kindness. Without an enemy.
> He loved, studied, preached, exemplified the
> Bible, and gloried in the Cross.

Rev. David Kimball was dismissed and his successor, Rev. Dana Goodsell, installed Sept. 27, 1837. Mr. Goodsell was inclined to be overbearing in his manner, and was not very popular. The following story is related. Some little time previous to his settlement, violins and one or two bass-viols had been introduced into the meeting-house gallery to assist the choir. It was necessary of course that these instruments should harmonize, and the players were in the habit of gathering in the gallery a short time pre-

HIS SUCCESSORS.

vious to the opening of service, and tuning their various instruments. Mr. Goodsell had not much knowledge of, and no ear for music. One Sabbath morning when they were tuning their instruments, as usual, Mr. Goodsell rose in the pulpit and raising his voice said, "I *insist* on that *preparation* being stopped." At noon when he started toward home for his dinner, David Shaw, one of the violin players, fell in a few rods behind him with his violin in hand, and following him through the street to his house, twanged out the lively notes of a march. Mr. Goodsell was dismissed Sept. 23, 1839. The next settled pastor was Rev. Wm. A. Hawley, who was installed July, 21, 1841, and dismissed Oct. 5, 1847. He was immediately succeeded by Rev. H. J. Gaylord, who served four years and was dismissed Oct. 6, 1851. Rev. D. B. Bradford was installed June 10, 1852, and dismissed May 17, 1854. From this time until January, 1858, the church had no permanent pastor. At this time the Rev. Solomon Clark commenced his labors and continued acting pastor until April, 1886, a period of over 28 years. His ministry was greatly blessed, he having received into the church during his pastorate here upwards of 150 members. Mr. Clark was never formally settled, but was hired from year to year. The church having had some trouble with previous pastors thought it a better policy not to settle another. From April, 1886, to April, 1888, the pulpit was supplied by Rev. F. G. Webster, who also preached at the same time at Cummington, where he resided. From May, 1888, to March, 1889, Rev. Geo. E. Spaulding supplied. At the latter date he was obliged to resign on account of ill health. In June, 1889, Rev. John A. Woodhull, by invitation, assumed the duties of acting pastor, and has continued in

PRESENT MEETING HOUSE AND TOWN HALL.

that position until the present time, to the general satisfaction of church and parish. He has quite recently received and accepted a call to become our settled pastor.

DEACONS.

The first deacons chosen were John Packard and James Richards, Nov. 15, 1792. Joseph Beals, April 29, 1803. He was the "Mountain Miller," the subject of a tract written by Rev. Wm. A. Hallock, which has had a worldwide circulation. Robert Beals, Sept. 23, 1813; Erastus Bates, June 27, 1828; John Carr, Sept. 6, 1834; Wm. N. Ford, Nov. 11, 1841; Freeman Hamlen, Aug. 30, 1844; Jerijah Barber, May 5, 1855; Wm. A. Bates, Nov. 16, 1867; Seth W. Clark and James A. Winslow, March 3, 1877. The last two named still hold the office.

PRESENT MEETING-HOUSE.

The first meeting-house was torn down and the present structure erected in 1846. The cost of the building was $2,450. It is believed that this was a great mistake, and that it would have been much less expensive to have remodeled the old meeting-house. The old frame was much heavier and stronger, and of more permanent character than that of the present building. This plan was favored by some at the time, but the majority favored a new building, and using the language of a local poetic genius:

"So down they tare
The house of prayer."

Early in 1890, the large pulpit was removed from the present edifice, and a handsome modern desk, the gift of Mrs. Woodhull, wife of the pastor, was placed on the platform. A low gallery for the choir was constructed at the rear of the platform where the old pulpit formerly stood. The present building originally had a very tall spire, which was blown off by a hard wind in the fall of 1859, and was replaced by one much lower.

DANIELS FUND.

In February, 1890, the parish was the recipient of over $1300 as a permanent fund, the income to be used to assist in sustaining preaching. The donor was Mr. Horace Daniels of Ashfield, a former resident.

ORGANIZATION OF FIRST PARISH.

Previous to 1838, no parish organization existed, all prudential matters being attended to by the town in their corporate capacity, the minister's salary and incidental expenses being voted in town meeting and assessed like other town charges. In that year the "First Parish and Religious Society" was organized and assumed these duties. It now numbers thirty members. The last original member deceased January 1, 1891, Mr. Roswell Davison. A Sunday School was first established here in 1819. The school is still in a flourishing condition, numbering about 100 members.

BAPTIST SOCIETY.

A Baptist Society was formed in the east part of the town, Feb. 25, 1833, the first meeting being called by Asa Thayer, under a warrant from Nehemiah Richards, Esq., of Cummington. The church was organized June 18, 1833, and consisted of 22 members. Their services were held at first in the brick school-house, but later a chapel was erected at the fork of the roads east of A. B. Cole's. Among those who have preached for the society were Elders McCullock, Eggleston, Kingsley, Newton, Pease, A. H. Sweet, and James Clark. Their first deacons were Asa Thayer and Jeremiah Stockwell. Jacob Jones, Jr. was afterwards chosen. The society finally became so weakened by deaths and removals, that services were discontinued and the organization was given up. The chapel was torn down and removed about 1870.

ADVENT CHAPEL.

The Adventists erected a chapel in the west part of the town near the North Pond and Henry S. Barton's, about 1882, where occasional services are held. There is no organized society.

CHAPTER V.

SCHOOLS.—FIRST LOCATION OF HOUSES.—NUMBER INCREASED.—REDUCED IN NUMBER AND RE-LOCATED.—"MOVING COMMITTEE."—INCIDENTS OF REMOVING.—DISTRICT SYSTEM.—LIST OF SCHOOL COMMITTEE.—STATISTICS.—NAMES OF PRESENT PUPILS IN THE PUBLIC SCHOOLS.

In April, 1788, the district "Voted to raise thirty pounds to be laid out in schooling the ensuing year;" also "Voted that the Selectmen be a Committee to divide the District into proper divisions for schooling." April 5, 1790, "Voted to build school-houses in each district for schooling. The town at first was divided into three districts, North, South, and West side of the brook. One school-house stood just south of the Shaw grove about midway between the brick store and the cemetery. The site can still be traced. One stood midway between Wm. H. Dyer's house and the brook on the north side of the road. The third stood where the present one on West Hill stands. This number was gradually increased until in 1837 the town had nine schools, besides one union school with Hawley. Their locations were as follows: The center house between the Town Hall and C. N. Dyer's store, neither being then in existence—one opposite J. O. Gloyd's—one at the corner east of David Packard's, on the north side—one a few rods west of Amos K. Griggs'—one at the corner near where Thaddeus Rood formerly lived—one on the West Cummington road, half a mile southwest of H. W. Beals'—one about midway between the Roswell Davison place and Edwin T. Torrey's,

FIRST LOCATION OF HOUSES.

on the west side—one near the intersection below Daniel Harris' in the extreme southwest part of the town—one where the Advent Chapel stands, near Henry S. Barton's. The union school-house was in Hawley, at the corner east of Mark E. Howes's. This number was sustained until 1868, when the town voted to abolish the school districts, or they were abolished by statute, and a Committee was appointed to reduce the number of schools and re-locate the school-houses. This reduction seemed necessary, as the number of legal scholars was only about 100. The Committee recommended five schools. The town finally voted six schools. The matter was only adjusted after much wrangling and numerous town meetings, and much ill feeling was engendered by the proposed changes. The following persons were chosen to superintend the removal and repair of the several school-houses, viz.: Joseph Sears, Francis W. Joy, Merritt Torrey, Russell Tirrell, Austin Cowing, and Homer Cook. This undertaking was an arduous one, but was successfully accomplished. The houses were placed on "runners" made of the trunks of large trees, and were drawn by oxen. These teams, together with such help as was needed, were furnished by the citizens gratuitously. A few teams in one or two instances were procured from out of town, which were paid for. The house near J. O. Gloyd's was removed to a location a few rods north of where it now stands, on the opposite side of the road. This site proving too wet, after a few years the frame was removed to the present location and newly covered, making practically a new house. This stands on the site of the Major David Whiton house, and is known as No. 2. The house west of A. K. Griggs' was removed to its present site, about 25 rods north of John F.

Cook's. During the night previous to the day set for its removal, the chains by which the oxen were to be attached to the building, were stolen, and no trace of them was ever discovered. This was quite a serious loss as the chains were extra heavy ones made especially for the purpose. Others were procured from out of town within two or three hours, and the building was removed to its new location before sundown of that day. This house is known as No. 3. It being impracticable to remove the house near H. S. Barton's, it was used for school purposes until 1880, when a new one to take its place, was built near Eugene Thatcher's. This is known as No. 4. The house which stood southeast of Daniel Harris' was removed to its present location north of H. Clark Packard's. This is known as No. 5. No school has been kept here for two or three years, the two or three scholars in this locality being provided by the town with school privileges at West Cummington and Windsor. The house which stood on the West Cummington road, southwest of the Wm. Robinson place, was removed to the ancient site east of C. W. Packard's, and is known as No. 6. Previous to the last named removal an attempt was made to remove the school-house which stood north of E. T. Torrey's to this location, it being much the better building. It was actually removed some 40 rods, but the number of teams being insufficient, it was decided to leave it until the next day. That night the building was fired and burned to the ground. All the houses, except No. 5, are provided with modern furniture, and are in good repair. Under the old system, each district was a corporation. School meetings were called in the same manner as town meetings. One person was chosen annually as Prudential Committee, with authority to contract with teachers, etc. Previous to 1840 from three to six persons were chosen annually by the town to serve with the minister as Examining School Committee. In that year it was voted that the Examining Committee consist of three persons, and that they be paid for their services. The following is a list of persons who have since held that office, the year first chosen and number of years service.

LIST OF SCHOOL COMMITTEE.

	First Chosen.	Years of Service.
Jason Richards,	1840	1
Albert Dyer,	"	13
Wm. N. Ford,	"	4
Levi N. Campbell,	1841	19
Rev. Wm. A. Hawley,	1842	10
Jason Tyrrell,	1843	2
S. S. Kingsley,	1845	1
Wm. Bassett,	"	2
Samuel Dyer,	1848	1
Samuel W. Lincoln,	1853	10
Jacob W. Pratt,	1854	3
Dr. Chas. Bowker,	1856	1
Edwin A. Atkins,	1857	4
Dr. John M. Eaton,	1859	2
Francis K. Cottrell,	1861	5
Seth W. Clark,	1863	13
Stephen Hayward, Jr.,	1865	3
Thaddeus Rood,	1866	4
James A. Winslow,	1867	21
J. Sebert Whitmarsh,	1871	3
Charles N. Dyer,	1872	10
E. Baxter Pratt,	1874	1

HISTORY OF PLAINFIELD.

	First Chosen.	Years of Service.
Lewis Shaw,	1875	3
Dr. Daniel E. Thayer,	1876	2
Frank A. Gurney,	1879	3
Sarah E. Howlett,	1880	1
James W. Loud,	"	9
Wm. C. Smith,	1889	1

The present board consists of Miss Azubah Howes, James A. Winslow and Charles N. Dyer.

One of the first, if not the first teacher employed, was Dea. James Richards, who taught a winter school in one part or another of the town for more than 30 years. As a rule, male teachers have been employed for winter and female for the summer and fall terms. Select schools have been occasionally taught during the fall months, the expense of which was met by tuition fees paid by the scholars. For some years the custom has been to have two terms, in the spring and fall, of three months each, in every school-house, No. 5 excepted, and a winter term in No. 1, which is attended by the larger pupils from all parts of the town. Since this arrangement, no select schools have been taught here. $784 were expended by the town the past year for schools, exclusive of school books and repairs. This was derived from the following sources: Raised by taxation, $450. Income of State School fund, $303.45. Dog fund refunded to the town, $40.53. The balance was used for repairs. The following is a list of pupils who have attended school in town from April, 1890, to April, 1891. Whole number, 89. Between 5 and 15, 75. Between 8 and 14, 45. Ages given were taken at beginning of school year.

LIST OF PUPILS.
School No. 1.

Name	AGE.	Name	AGE.
Arthur H. Atkins,	17	Mary E. Winslow,	16
Belle S. Barton,	17	Hermie S. Butler,	13
Alice L. Billings,	16	Clara D. C. Butler,	9
Estella M. Cleveland,	14	Richard D. Butler,	6
Bessie B. Denio,	11	Helen R. Dunham,	5
Grace E. Dyer,	14	C. Frederick Dyer.	7
L. Genevieve Dyer,	10	Anna M. King,	5
Clara A. Dunham,	11	Charles R. King,	5
F. Hallie Holden,	12	Bell Morse,	5
P. W. Hitchcock, Hawley	18	Ensign Morse, Jr.,	4
Robert M. Sears,	13	Minnie B. Packard,	6
Anna G. Sears,	11	Hattie G. Parker,	10
Alvah E. Stetson,	20	Julia Smith,	8
Albert E. Stetson,	17	Florence Stetson,	13
Mary E. Shaw,	15	Harry J. Stetson,	9
Robert L. Streeter,	16	Hilda Swanson,	8
Rosa M. Streeter,	14	Nina L. Veber,	10

School No. 2.

Name	AGE.	Name	AGE.
Agnes M. Fenton,	11	Herbert T. Kinney,	13
Helen B. Fenton,	9	Albert N. Lincoln,	10
Lucy A. Gloyd,	14	Fred Lincoln,	8
Joseph A. Gloyd,	12	Jane A. Loud,	15
Mary A. Gloyd,	10	Mary E. Loud,	12
Enos R. Hawks,	15	Angus C. Loud,	10
Arthur J. Hawks,	12	Bertie S. Longley,	11
Alden C. Holden,	11	Edith G. Shaw,	10

Herbert H. Willcutt, 11.

School No 3.

	AGE.		AGE.
Bertie L. Billings,	13	Frank E. Green,	9
Lucy E. Billings,	11	Clara C. Scott, (Hawley,)	8
Ezra P. Billings,	7	Ralph L. Scott, (do.)	6
Frank W. Dyer,	13	Fordyce A. Thayer,	16
Willie H. Dyer,	11	Willis D. Thayer,	14
Sadie A. Dyer,	8	Clara L. Thayer,	8
Carrie E. Gardner,	7	Chas. A. Tirrell,	6
Florence M. Gardner,	5	Clarence W. Tirrell,	5

School No. 4.

	AGE.		AGE.
Ellen A. Blanchard,	14	Lottie A. Ingrahm,	11
Edna R. Blanchard,	8	Lillian C. Mason,	11
George A. Blanchard,	14	Harold E. Mason,	8

Charles E. Thatcher, 6.

School No. 5.

	AGE.		AGE.
Robert Mason,	14	Theodore Meekins,	11
Daughter of Thos. Mason —		Schooled at Windsor.	
Schooled at W. Cummington.			

School No. 6.

	AGE.		AGE.
Blanche L. Cudworth,	7	Susan G. Streeter,	7
Adelbert N. Dyer,	13	Allie M. Streeter,	6
Mary E. Hammond,	12	Walter E. Streeter,	4
John H. Packard,	7	Willie Taylor,	11
Maggie A. Packard,	6	Mabel A. Torrey,	6
Joseph W. Packard,	5	G. Herbert Vincent,	5

We note with pleasure, that in the last ten years, the number of pupils has increased from 60 to 89.

CHAPTER VI.

TOWN HALL.—ROADS.—EARLY MODES OF TRAVEL.—LOST IN THE WOODS.—EARLY BRIDGE BUILDING.—PRESENT SYSTEM OF REPAIRING ROADS.—ROAD COMMISSIONERS.—NAMES OF STREETS.—POST OFFICES.—POSTMASTERS.—FIRST MAIL SUPPLY. --PRESENT MAIL FACILITIES.—EARLY RATES OF POSTAGE.

The Town Hall was erected in 1847. It was built by the late Capt. James Cook, by contract, for $900, five-ninths of it being paid by the town, and four-ninths by the center school district. The first floor, with the exception of a small room used for keeping the town weights and measures and for the storage of books, was occupied for school purposes. The school at that time was graded, and two teachers were employed at least a portion of the year. The larger school room occupied the entire north end, the smaller one being in the southeast corner, with a room between for storing wood. In 1872, two rooms being no longer necessary, the small room was doubled in size by removing partitions, and has since been used as the only school room. The old room at the north end was divided by a partition, the east part being used for a wood room, and the west part was given to the church and parish to be used for prayer meetings and other gatherings, it being fitted up by the ladies for that purpose. The hall was painted last year (1890) both inside and out, and the interior papered in an artistic manner. A portion of the floor was carpeted with oil cloth.

ROADS.

It is very probable that quite a number of roads had been laid out in the district while it was a part of Cummington. These were most of them mere bridle paths, as wheel vehicles with the exception of ox carts were rare. The ordinary mode of travel was on foot or horseback. If a grist was to be taken to the mill, it was slung across the horse's back and given in charge of a boy who was placed on top. On Sundays, a "pillion" was placed behind the saddle which the "goodman" bestrode, while his wife standing on the "horse block" nimbly mounted the pillion, perchance with a baby in her arms, and clinging to her husband they wended their way to the meeting-house, the larger children following on foot. If they were fortunate enough to possess a half-broken colt, this would probably be proudly ridden by one of the older boys. It must be remembered that the first roads laid out were not where the principal roads are now. Some of them are now unimportant, and many were long since discontinued. It is related that about the year 1800, Mrs. Polly White, mother of the late O. S. White, then a young married woman of about 18, and who was settled with her husband on the homestead so long occupied by them in the south part of the town, started to visit a neighbor, Mrs. Samuel Streeter, who lived where S. H. Sears now lives, something over a mile distant. At that time the town was mostly covered with woods, and for a portion of the way the path was indicated by marked trees. She missed the way and wandered in the woods for an hour or less, when she heard at some distance the cheerful notes of a dinner horn blown by Mrs. Streeter to call the men to dinner, and directing her steps toward the welcome sound, she soon reached the house, we may presume in time for dinner. The roads were rapidly improved, and new ones were every year constructed. Soon after this the "thorough brace" wagon was introduced, which was thought to be the height of perfection. If a journey of any length was to be taken with it, a small kettle of tar was hung from the hind axle to be used for lubricating purposes, it being thought necessary to apply it as often as once in ten miles.

BRIDGES.

March 22, 1790, "Voted that Simon Burroughs, Caleb White and Jeremiah Robinson be a committee to view the ground near Streeter's Saw-mill and Determine whether it be necessary to build a bridge over the Brook just above said mill or not." Later at the same meeting it was voted to build the bridge, which was probably one of the first in town. After the meeting-house was built, several new roads were very soon laid to accommodate the inhabitants in attending church. The town is fortunate in having no long bridges to support. Mill Brook is spanned by four. The most expensive bridge is the one known as "High Bridge," near Wm. H. Packard's. The stream at this place is narrow but 25 or 30 feet below the road bed. This bridge is of stone with culvert for the passage of the water, with a superstructure of wood. It has been necessary to rebuild this several times within the memory of the writer.

METHODS OF REPAIR OF ROADS.

There are $42\frac{5}{8}$ miles of road in town, now used. In 1885 the town purchased a "Victor" Road machine, which is successfully used in repairing most of the roads. If properly used an excellent road is the result. The mounds or water bars, formerly so numerous and annoying to the traveler, have mostly disappeared since the machine has been used. The roads are kept in repair by an annual appropriation averaging about $800, while $300 is appropriated for breaking roads in winter. The roads were formerly divided into 19 or 20 highway districts, each under the supervision of a highway surveyor. The Legislature of 1889 abolished this office, and all towns were required to have a Superintendent of Streets, appointed by the Selectmen, or a board of three Road Commissioners. The town accepted the latter alternative and chose Warren I. Dunham, A. N. Gurney and J. O. Gloyd. It is the general opinion that for farming communities the old system was preferable. At the annual meeting in March, 1891, this board was abolished, and W. I. Dunham was appointed Superintendent of Streets by the Selectmen.

NAMES OF STREETS.

By an act of the Legislature of 1877, the Selectmen were required to name all roads on which any person lived, and specify the name of the street on which each voter lives, both on the Register of Voters, and on posted lists of the same. They are as follows:—

Bow, from Main to Grant, by S. Burt's.
Broome, from Central to Pleasant, by O. C. Burt's.
Bluff, from Prospect to Summit, by H. W. Beals'.
Central, from Hawley line past M. C. Butler's, J. W. Sears' and W. E. Shaw's, to Cummington line.
East, from Main to Grant, by J. A. Winslow's.
Governor, from Prospect to Summit, by C. W. Packard's.
Grant, from Hawley line to Ashfield line, by Z. F. Cook's.

NAMES OF STREETS.

Hawley, from Main to Hawley line, by N. Barton's.
High, from River to Cummington, by A. N. Gurney's.
Hill, from Main to River, by C. F. Dunham's.
Liberty, from Prospect to terminus, by M. Stetson's.
Lincoln, from River to High, by N. W. Cook's.
Main, from Savoy line by Onslow Taylor's and the Center of the town, past L. E. Parker's, to Ashfield line.
Maple, from Summit by O. Tirrell's, to terminus.
Mountain, from Prospect by M. Torrey's, to terminus.
North, from Central by A. L. Richmond's, to Ashfield line.
Parsons Avenue, from Central east to its terminus.
Pleasant, from Central by L. K. Thayer's, to Ashfield line.
Prospect, from Main by S. Stetson's, and W. M. Cleveland's, to Cummington line.
River, from Main by G. W. King's and Lester E. Streeter's, to Cummington line.
South, from Pleasant by L. W. Gloyd's, to Cummington line.
Stetson Avenue, from Main north by H. S. Barton's, to Hawley line.
Summit, from Prospect to High, by Alden E. Streeter's.
Union, from Central, near the cemetery, by S. H. Sears' and J. F. Gurney's, to River.
West, from Main by H. Clark Packard's, to Cummington line.
Windsor Av., from West by D. Harris', to Windsor line.

POST OFFICES AND POST MASTERS.

A Post Office was established here in 1816, with John Mack as Post Master. He held the office during his lifetime and was succeeded by John Mack, Jr., and Whitney Hitchcock. After him the office was held by

Abner Gurney, who kept it in his store in the L part of the Moses Hallock house. He was succeeded by Leavitt Hallock. He kept it for a time in his house, the same now occupied by Mrs. Hamlen. Jacb Clark, Leonard Campbell and Levi Clark each afterward held the office. In 1856 Leonard Campbell was again appointed, and held the office over 30 years until 1886, when he resigned and Foster W. Gilbert was appointed and assumed the office, Oct. 1, 1886. He tendered his resignation March 5, 1889, and Charles N. Dyer, the present incumbent, was commissioned June 18, 1889. The first mail supply was from Cummington, and was carried on foot by Kingman Thayer, who made the trip once a week, bringing the mail bag on his back. This route was afterward extended to Shelburne Falls through Hawley and Buckland, and two trips per week were made. Later a route was established from South Deerfield to South Adams, through this town, on which four-horse coaches were run, going out one day and returning the next. When first established, the present county road had not been laid. The stage when coming from Ashfield ascended the hill just east of Samuel and Lot Bassett's in Ashfield, passing the house, then on by William Ford's and where Dea. Winslow lives, thence to the village, and down the hill by S. C. Streeter's,—up the stream over a section of road now discontinued, then by Marshall Stetson's over the now discontinued road by the Allis place, which intersected the present county road near Henry S. Barton's. In 1885 a route was established between Plainfield and Charlemont on the Fitchburg R. R., through East Hawley, to run daily and return, by which route the larger part of the mail is sent and received. We are also supplied by a route running every other day

EARLY RATES OF POSTAGE.

from Ashfield to Adams, returning the next day. The early postal rates were as follows: For distances not over 80 miles, 6¼c—80 to 150, 12½c—150 to 400, 18¾c—over 400, 25c. Prepayment optional. The method of conducting the business of the post office 50 years ago, made it much more complicated and vexatious than under the present system.

CHAPTER VII.

CEMETERIES.—BILL OF MORTALITY.—LIST OF AGED DECEASED.—SUICIDES.—SUDDEN DEATHS.

The place earliest used in town for a cemetery, so far as known, was the lot on the west side of the road, just north of Mrs. Rachel Shaw's, now occupied by C. W. Streeter as a pasture. Scarcely any trace of these early burials, of which there were only a few, now remains. No headstones were erected. Another ancient cemetery lies on the east side of the road just south of the meeting-house. This was in general use for perhaps twenty years, but was long since abandoned. The last interment here was that of Daniel Streeter, who suicided in 1855. Here were interred Jeremiah Robinson, who owned and operated the first corn mill in town, and his successor, Joseph Beals, the "Mountain Miller," and their families. These last named have been re-interred in the principal cemetery north of the meeting-house. In 1889, the writer witnessed the disinterment of the remains of Jeremiah Robinson, who died in 1824. Portions of the coffin still remained. One fragment bore his initials, J. R., formed by brass-headed nails driven into the wood, as was the custom in those days. Some 20 headstones bearing inscriptions still remain.—About twenty persons were buried in the pasture about half a mile north of Amos K. Griggs'. No headstones were erected, but the graves can still be distinctly traced.—

There is another old burial ground about a mile northwest of Marshall Stetson's, on the old stage road now discontinued. Here quite a number of headstones are still standing. Among those interred here, is the wife of Lemuel Allis, a Revolutionary pensioner.—On the farm of the late Dexter Dyer, in the extreme southwest part of the town, is a small yard where one or two families are buried. —Near Dea. Winslow's, in the east part of the town, is another, formerly used by the Stockwell family. Here are a few graves, most of them marked by headstones.—A few persons were buried in what is now a pasture, south of P. H. Cudworth's, their graves being marked by headstones with inscriptions.—A cemetery was early opened in the southeast part of the town, near Wm. H. Dyer's. This yard is nearly filled, most of the graves being marked with headstones or monuments. Here are buried Capt. James Hayward, Abram and Jacob Clark, Elijah Warner, Sr., and Maj. David Whiton, who were among the first settlers. It is enclosed by a stone wall, and is neatly kept and cared for by Mr. Dyer.—In the southwest part of the town is another yard which has been cared for by Orrin Tirrell. This is well enclosed, and contains the handsome monument erected to the memory of the late Orrin Tirrell, Sr., as well as many other respectable headstones. The principal cemetery of the town, which lies about $\frac{1}{3}$ of a mile north of the meeting-house, was opened in 1808. The first person buried there was Lieut. Solomon Shaw. This yard was enlarged in 1856, and enclosed by a handsome stone wall. This is now used almost exclusively by persons from all parts of the town as a burial-place. Here are interred the Rev. Moses Hallock, Dr. Jacob Porter, Dea. James Richards, John Mack, Dr. Samuel Shaw, Samuel Streeter,

Leavitt Hallock, and many others prominent in the history of the town. A receiving tomb was built in the northwest corner of the yard in 1884, by the town, and is used during the winter months. We regret that the yard is not cared for as it should be. It is proposed to organize a Cemetery Association, composed of a number of our citizens, who would be authorized to control it, and by whom it might be enlarged and properly laid out. A small fee would be charged for burial lots, which have heretofore been free, the income from which would be used in caring for and beautifying the grounds. It is hoped that the project will be promptly carried out, as it is necessary that the grounds be enlarged within a year or two, and every citizen should be interested in it.

*   *   *   *   *   *

>In that village on the hill
>Never is sound of smithy or mill;
>The houses are thatched with grass and flowers,
>Never a clock to tell the hours;
>The marble doors are always shut;
>You may not enter at hall or hut.
>All the village lie asleep,
>Never a grain to sow or reap;
>Never in dreams to moan or sigh—
>Silent, and idle, and low, they lie.
>
>In that village *under* the hill,
>When the night is starry and still,
>Many a weary soul in prayer
>Looks to the other village there,
>And weeping and sighing, longs to go
>Up to that home from this below;
>Longs to sleep by the forest wild,
>Whither have vanished wife and child,
>And heareth, praying, the answer fall,—
>" Patience: That village shall hold you all!"
>
> *Rose Terry Cooke.*

BILL OF MORTALITY.

So live that when thy summons comes to join
The innumerable caravan that moves
To that mysterious realm where each shall take
His chamber in the silent halls of death,
Thou go not like the quarry slave at night,
Scourged to his dungeon; but, sustained and soothed
By an unfaltering trust, approach thy grave
Like one who wraps the drapery of his couch
About him, and lies down to pleasant dreams.
Bryant.

BILL OF MORTALITY.

This town is regarded as a very healthy locality, and 58 per cent. of the deaths in the last 25 years, have been of persons over 70 years of age. The early church records furnish by far the most complete list of deaths for the period which they cover. Unfortunately in the church records the ages are not given till 1802. Dr. Porter says, "The following table exhibits the most complete list that I have been able to obtain of the deaths from 1785, inclusive, to the present time, with the name and age of the oldest person who died in each year from 1802." His list ends with the year 1833, and has been continued by the writer up to the present year:

1785	2		1794	18
1786	2		1795	2
1787	8		1796	11
1788	6		1797	8
1789	2		1798	0
1790	3		1799	10
1791	6		1800	13
1792	7		1801	18
		1793 3		
1802	9	Widow Macintire,		83
1803	30	John Carr,		94
1804	15	Jacob Gloyd,		71

1805	11	Dea. John Packard's wife,	60
1806	15	Widow Whiton,	86
1807	14	Dea. John Packard,	71
1808	18	Moses Curtis,	86
1809	8	Jacob Hawes,	68
1810	15	Widow Snow,	81
1811	11	Seth Ford's wife,	86
1812	12	Jacob Joy,	77
1813	17	Dea. Joseph Beals,	61
1814	16	Ebenezer Beals,	83
1815	13	Jepthah Pool's wife,	60
1816	11	Widow Hannah Colson,	96
1817	12	Caleb Beals,	60
1818	14	Widow Hannah Smith,	75
1819	14	Widow Shaw,	81
1820	7	John Joy's wife,	39
1821	12	Benjamin Pool,	56
1822	10	Widow Daniels,	76
1823	13	Joseph Pool,	84
1824	15	Samuel Whitman,	93
1825	13	Dea. Gideon Shaw,	80
1826	16	Levi Stetson,	80
1827	8	Caleb Joy,	76
1828	9	Ammon White,	82
1829	13	Noah Packard's wife,	75
1830	17	Benjamin Carr's wife,	82
1831	13	Widow Abigail Vining,	71
1832	7	Jacob Clark,	77
1833	9	Gideon Hammond,	90
1834	15	Abraham Clark,	83
1835	6	Ebenezer Bisbee's wife,	78
1836	10	Widow of Andrew Cook,	96

BILL OF MORTALITY.

1837	13	James Dyer,	95
1838	12	Benjamin Carr,	92
1839	11	Widow Silence Clark,	83
1840	9	Caleb White,	96
1841	11	Mary Ann Noyes,	34
1842	21	Dea. James Richards,	85
1843	13	Paul McCoy,	85
1844	16	Samuel Streeter,	90
1845	9	Daniel Gurney,	80
1846	12	Ebenezer Dickinson,	94
1847	15	Barnabas Packard,	83
1848	10	Olive Torrey,	85
1849	14	Sarah Beals,	90
1850	22	Sally Warner,	85
1851	19	Vincent Curtis,	91
1852	17	John Hamlen,	89
1853	17	Jacob Snow,	94
1855	12	Elizabeth Hayward,	87
1856	9	Alice Gloyd,	86
1857	12	Lois Nash,	92
1858	17	Sally Beals,	88
1859	8	Whitcomb Stetson,	84
1860	8	Jacob Beals,	77
1861	10	Jacob Jones, Sr.,	90
1862	12	Samuel Davison,	88
1863	22	Polly Holdridge,	85
1864	11	Esther Baldwin,	98
1865	8	Consider Stockwell,	74

From 1866, for comparison, the number of *births* occurring in each year is placed at the left of date.

7	1866	9	Sally Dyer,	73
11	1867	10	Polly Shaw,	93

14	1868	8	Levi Cook,	85
12	1869	12	Nancy Pease,	90
13	1870	9	Polly Tirrell,	95
6	1871	10	Samuel White,	94
9	1872	6	Jacob Whitmarsh,	83
8	1873	8	Julia Butler,	85
10	1874	11	Levi Campbell,	88
4	1875	2	Sally Bradley,	72
7	1876	6	James Joy,	82
7	1877	8	Samuel Thayer, Jr.,	88
6	1878	5	Abigail Torrey,	82
11	1879	9	John Bisbee,	93
5	1880	9	Hannah Cook,	87
6	1881	12	Stephen Hayward,	94
7	1882	12	Jerusha King,	93
3	1883	13	Samuel Loud,	88
5	1884	12	David Shaw,	90
4	1885	7	Sally Packard,	91
9	1886	4	Ezra W. Haskins,	85
6	1887	10	Delia Warner,	87
6	1888	7	Mary Joy,	91
8	1889	8	Seth S. Williams,	87
3	1890	7	James Warner,	91

Total births in last 25 years, 187. Deaths, 214. The greatest age attained by any person was 98, Esther Baldwin in 1864. In 1794 and 1803 the scarlet fever prevailed; in 1806, the typhus fever. In 1798 there were no deaths. In 1834, 11 of the 15 deaths were children under 5 years of age, and it does not appear that there was any prevalent disease. In 1850, dysentery prevailed, there being 15 deaths from that cause. On Aug. 29 of that year, three children lay dead, and also on Sept. 15.—Oct. 7, 1857,

SUDDEN DEATHS.   63

three adults died, viz.: Phebe Hitchcock, Beza Reed and Sarah Jones. Their funerals were attended on the same day, Oct. 9.—May 7, 1855, Daniel Streeter suicided by hanging himself to a tree in the woods near the southeast corner of Stephen Parsons' farm.—April 5, 1873, Dr. G. H. Taylor took his own life by hanging himself in his barn. The following deaths seem worthy of particular notice: Jan. 9, 1804, Lucinda Packard was found dead in her bed. May 19, 1804, James Thayer was drowned at Cummington, aged 21. June 22, 1812, Levi Stetson, Jr., aged 35, was killed almost instantly by the fall of a tree. Aug. 11, 1812, the wife of Gideon Hammond died in her chair at work, instantly, as is supposed. Her husband awoke from a short nap after dinner, and found her sitting at her quill-wheel, dead. Her age was 51. Oct. 22, 1817, a son of Jetson Stetson died from a bean in the windpipe, aged 5. May 4, 1820, Daniel Brown was killed instantly by a log rolling over him. May 10, 1828, the wife of Benjamin Towne, aged 39, was found after a long search by many persons, dead in the woods in Hawley, having wandered from home several days before, while insane. Oct. 28, 1831, Clarissa Stetson, aged 8, died in consequence of burns received from her clothes taking fire. July 11, 1833, Samuel Swift, aged about 50, was killed instantly at Cummington by the fall of a tree. March 8, 1834, Charles Bela Dyer, 2 years old, died in consequence of a piece of apple in the windpipe. Jan. 30, 1842, Matthias Crittenden, aged 60, fell dead while returning from attending church. Marcus M. Lincoln, aged 7, son of Isaac K. Lincoln, was drowned July 15, 1845, while bathing with other boys in a small pond, west of Joseph Gloyd's. Dec. 19, 1880, Joseph Gloyd, Jr., aged 74, died very suddenly. He rose in the morning as usual and had partially dressed, when he complained of feeling ill, and expired in a few moments. Dec. 16, 1886, Joseph Sears, aged 66, died suddenly of heart disease. He had just returned from a neighbors, apparently in his usual health. He sat down on entering the house, being somewhat out of breath, and soon after expired. John Joy fell, or was thrown from his horse, on the hill above Nelson W. Cook's, breaking his neck, Aug. 21, 1848, while on his way to church. His age was 69. Jacob Jones, Jr. died suddenly while at work near his barn, Dec. 15, 1873, aged 71.

CHAPTER VIII.

STORES AND MANUFACTURES.—JOHN MACK.—I. K. LINCOLN AND OTHERS.—JACOB AND LEVI CLARK.—LEONARD CAMPBELL.—STORES AT PRESENT TIME.—ROBINSON'S CORN MILL.—WARNER, WHITING & CO.—STREETER'S FACTORY.—TANNERY.—OTHER MANUFACTURES.

Tradition says that one Perkins kept the first store in town, but his given name and place of business are not known. His business was probably unimportant, else some account of it would have been handed down. With the above exception, the first store established was that of John Mack, some time previous to 1816. The building used stood a rod or two south of Clark Smith's house. About 1820 he erected the brick store on the common, now occupied by H. S. Packard. This was considered a very elegant structure at that time, and is really a fine, substantial building. Here he did business until his death in 1833. He was for some ten years or more the only merchant in town and did a thriving business. The goods kept 75 years ago were very few in number and variety. Liquors of various kinds, molasses, salt, codfish, a little brown and loaf sugar, chintz cloth, and possibly one or two other kinds, thread, etc. Isaac K. Lincoln built a store in the southeast part of the town, and carried on the mercantile business for some 20 years. Much of the trade was an exchange business. Eggs, cheese, tow and linen cloth were taken in exchange for goods. These commodities were taken by teams to Boston, which returned loaded with goods for the store. It took about eight days to make the round trip. Iram Packard built the house now occupied by Levi Clark as early as 1825, a portion of which he used as a store. This was afterwards kept by Aaron Sawyer, and about 1839 by Shaw & Stowell; then by Jacob and Levi Clark. Mr. Clark discontinued the business in 1855. G. G. Keyes afterwards leased the rooms and kept a store there from about 1859 to 1862 or 3. Lyman Dawes also had a store there for a short time. Leonard Campbell opened a store here in 1855 in the building formerly occupied by Ira Hamlen, as a hatter's shop. In a few years he enlarged the building, and has continued in business until the present time. For nearly 20 years this was the only store in town, except while Keyes and Dawes were here, which was only a short time. For some 25 years up to about 1875, and even later, the palm-leaf hat industry was a profitable part of the merchant's business. This was carried on mostly by the Messrs. Clark and later by Mr. Campbell. The prepared leaf was furnished by the merchants, and by them given out to the different families. The hats were braided by the women and girls, and although the pay was small, it amounted in the aggregate to quite a large sum. At one time probably three-fourths of the families in town were engaged in the business. Mr. Campbell for about 25 years made a specialty of the millinery business, in which he had a heavy trade from this and adjoining towns. He was in trade here a few years previous to 1855, but discontinued the business for awhile, and re-opened that year. Abner Gurney kept a store for a short time in the L part of the house formerly occupied by Rev. Mr. Hallock, the post office being kept there at the same time. The business of John Mack was

STORES AT PRESENT TIME. 67

carried on by John Mack, Jr. for a year or two when it was bought by Whitney J. Hitchcock. He was not here long, and was succceeded by Shaw & Stowell. Afterward W. C. Gilbert bought and carried on the store for some years, or until about 1852, when he left it for a farm. Then Charles Mack, who had been clerk for Gilbert, bought the stock and carried on the business for two or three years. Then S. W. Streeter took the business, and after him E. A. Clark and Eugene Shaw were in it for a short time; but the business was closed up in 1856. No store was kept here from this time until about 1873, when the store was purchased by Chas. R. Burt, who stocked it with goods and carried on the business for some four years, when he sold out to Mrs. Eliza A. Packard, who kept the store with the assistance of her sons for about seven years, when the business was transferred to her oldest son, H. S. Packard, by whom it has since been conducted. He has lately enlarged the main store room (which had been divided by C. R. Burt) and filled it with a large and complete stock of goods. C. N. Dyer opened a small grocery store in his house in 1880. The business increasing, other lines of goods were added, and interior changes in the building were made to accommodate it. When F. W. Gilbert was appointed postmaster in 1886, the post office was removed to this store and placed in charge of Mr. Dyer, who was Asst. P. M. In 1887 Mr. Dyer sold the place, including the farm, and bought of D. H. Gould the corner lot east of the Town Hall, on which he at once erected a building to be used for a store and tenement, to which he removed his business, including the post office, about Sept. 1, 1887, and where he still carries it on. There are several dealers in farmers' produce. L. W. Joy, who has been in the business many years, and disposes of his produce in Northampton; A. N. Gurney, who carries his produce to Adams, his specialty being pork in the whole carcass, which he sells to retail dealers; he also sells flour, meal, etc., and some heavy groceries. J. N. Benjamin also does a produce business, disposing of his stock at Adams. His specialties are butter, whole pork, and apples.

MANUFACTURES.

[The author is largely indebted to an article in the Hampshire Co. Gazetteer, by F. W. Gilbert, for the substance of this article.]

It is believed that the grist mill, or "corn mill," as it was called, of Jeremiah Robinson, said to have been established in 1789, and the saw mill of Samuel Streeter, both on Mill brook, were the first mills of any kind established here, being mentioned in the records as early as 1791. In 1798 the grist mill was purchased by Joseph Beals, "the Mountain Miller," who managed the business until his death in 1813. His son, Dea. Robert, then conducted it for a number of years, and about 1827 or 1828 built the present mill, which stands several rods further down the stream than the original structure. Jared Bisbee, Horatio Lyon, Dexter White and Edwin Torrey succeeded in turn to the management. In 1861 James A. Nash purchased the property. He has greatly improved it and still carries on the business. Samuel Streeter's saw-mill stood just above the site of Streeter's factory. A saw-mill operated by his sons and grandson, also his great-grandson, was continued on the same site until about 1870. On the brook in the northeast corner of the town is a saw-mill. The original mill on this site was built by Levi Campbell, and was for many years operated by his son, Levi N. Campbell.

MANUFACTURES.

MILL OF "THE MOUNTAIN MILLER."

About 1884 or 1885 it came into the possession of George W. Billings. He substituted a circular mill for the old style, and carried on the business until the mill was burned in April, 1890. Mr. Billings has rebuilt it, and purchased new machinery. His specialty is the manufacture of cloth boards. The stream which runs near Wm. H. Dyer's has been from early times the scene of many attempts at manufacture, most of them being for the time successful. Probably the first enterprise of this sort was the grist mill of Thomas Shaw, which was situated some distance north of W. H. Dyer's, near the old brickyard. Evidence exists that places the date of its erection before 1800. It was abandoned about 1830, and no trace of it remains. Who first opened the brickyard near it is uncertain, but brick were made there early in the present century, probably by Joshua or Thomas Shaw. The Warner brothers made brick there for several years in the vicinity of 1840 and later. About 1871 or 1872 O. S. White and S. W. Clark re-fitted the yard and made brick for two or three seasons; since then none have been made there. On the stream just below this in the earlier part of the century was the cloth dressing shop of Jacob Clark. About 1830, on nearly the same site, Randall Whiting, James and Cushing Warner, under the firm name of Warner, Whiting & Co., built a factory for the manufacture of satinets, and for general custom work. A boarding-house was also erected. About a dozen hands were employed in the factory. After some years the firm failed and the business was suspended. Subsequently, Wm. Gurney made an attempt to revive the business, but without much success. The buildings were removed about 1857. The site of the factory was about six rods south of the road on

MANUFACTURES.

the west side of the stream, near W. H. Dyer's. Remnants of the dam and raceway are still visible. Still lower on the stream, John White built a mill for the manufacture of broom handles about 1836. This was in operation for eight or ten years, and the buildings were then removed. A saw-mill on the same site was continued a few years longer. Further down was the ancient saw-mill of Ziba White. This mill was probably erected soon after 1800, and was in use about 40 years. A mill privilege below this was improved by Warner & Gloyd about 1845. They erected a saw-mill, and afterwards a cider mill. The saw-mill was not used after 1856, and both were soon afterwards torn down. The small stream by the side of the road just below Campbell's store seems hardly sufficient to turn a boy's water-wheel, yet on this rivulet, about 65 years ago, a pretentious tannery was erected by Dorn & Remington. Their water-wheel was an overshot, of unusual size, 18 feet in diameter, and their buildings were quite capacious. The preparations proved unavailable, and they went down the valley, and settled on Mill Brook. On this brooklet at about the same time were the potash works of Iram Packard. At the time Dorn & Remington removed to the valley, in 1830, they built a large tannery 100x30, covering 80 vats, nearly opposite the present residence of Lester Streeter, where they did a large business. Mr. Dorn sold his share to a Mr. Parsons, and later the new firm disposed of the property to Giddings & Latham. After a time Giddings disposed of his share to Latham, who carried on the business until his death in 1851. The business was not afterward revived. The beam house was fitted up for the manufacture of broom handles a number of years later by Nelson C. Clapp, but not much was done at the business. On the small brooklet referred to near the village, before Dorn & Remington began their preparations there, Cyrus Joy had a small tannery for tanning upper leather. There was also about that time, a small tannery a few rods east of Homer Cook's. There were but a few vats, and no water power, the bark being ground at Samuel Streeter's saw-mill and drawn up the hill to the tannery. At the upper water privilege on Mill Brook, Isaiah Stetson, in 1817, built a saw-mill and managed it for several years. Afterwards David and Wm. Stowell purchased it, and continued the business until 1854, at which date it passed into the hands of W. C. Gilbert. In 1855, George W. King bought, and still owns the property. He manufactures broom and brush handles, besides custom sawing and planing.—Adjoining Samuel Streeter's saw-mill, before referred to, in the early part of the century was a cloth-dressing shop conducted successively by Daniel Richards, Mr. Gleason and others. On the site of this, in 1820, Arnold and Nahum Streeter built a factory for the manufacture of satinet, flannel, and other woolen goods. This was burned in 1825. It was rebuilt and managed by the Streeter family until 1876, when it was again destroyed by fire, and has not been rebuilt.—On the other side of the road from Willcutt's saw-mill, in 1810 was a flax-dressing mill, owned and run by Noah and Iram Packard. About 1816, Reuben Hamlen and Otis Pratt built on the same site a factory for the manufacture of satinets and woolen goods. In 1820 the building which is now the Willcutt mill was removed across the road where it now stands. Mr. Pratt sold his share to Erastus Bates, who moving West in 1834 left Mr. Hamlen to manage the mill alone. After a few years the business was given up. Later, Jason

Noyes used it for a chair factory. Elbridge King rented it for awhile. Capt. James Cook finally bought the property, and it was used for a saw-mill. He sold to Daniel Ingraham, who made baskets there. In 1867 William Willcutt bought the plant from Ingraham, repaired it thoroughly and put in entirely new machinery, including a circular saw-mill. He now uses annually from 30 to 50 thousand feet of hard wood lumber in the manufacture of whip butts, which are sold in Westfield, Mass. He also makes some broom and brush handles, besides doing custom sawing and planing. Several men are employed. His son, George L., has an interest in the business.—A few rods below the present grist-mill of J. A. Nash, was once a saw-mill, long since abandoned. Portions of the foundation walls are still visible. In 1852 Wm. J. Shattuck built a saw-mill on the west branch of Mill brook. The supply of water proving insufficient, the mill was after several years practically abandoned, and the building was removed in 1884.—The saw-mill at the outlet of the crooked pond in the extreme northwest part of the town, now owned by Onslow Taylor, was built by Lyman Morton, more than fifty years ago. A circular mill was put in by the present owner a few years since. Mr. Morton also built a dam on the " Grant " brook near David Packard's, and erected a small shop there about 1825. The power was used for operating a trip-hammer for forging heavy iron work. Isaac Saddler, more than 60 years ago, had a cloth-dressing shop on Mill Brook, near the residence of the late Philander Packard. Later Homan Hallock had a shop near by, where he manufactured Arabic type, using the same water power. In 1840 there was a tack shop near where Shepard Dyer lives, conducted by Roland Shaw, where six or eight men were employed. No power was used. Tacks were also made in a shop at the upper village not far from the same time. Early in the present century, Ira Hamlen operated a hatter's shop, which together with his house was burnt in 1824. It was rebuilt, and business carried on for some time. The building used is now the south wing of Campbell's store.

CHAPTER IX.

PHYSICIANS.--DR. TORREY.--DR. PORTER.--DR. SAMUEL SHAW.—"HIT HIM ANOTHER."—LATER PRACTITIONERS.--JUSTICES OF THE PEACE.

The first physician practising in town was Dr. Solomon Bond, his name occurring in the town records as early as 1789. He was succeeded by Dr. Barney Torrey and Dr. Jacob Porter. The latter, although a highly educated man, gave his attention mostly to literary pursuits, being well versed in botany and mineralogy. His medical practice was very inconsiderable. He was the author of a history of Plainfield, published in 1834. He died Nov. 15, 1846, aged 63. He was interred near the front of the principal cemetery under the shade of six tamerack trees which he had set out there some years previous. They have since been removed. All the young trees of that variety in the cemetery and vicinity sprung from seed from these six trees, as it was scattered by the winds.

DR. SAMUEL SHAW,

who spent his life here, deserves more than a passing notice. He was a son of Josiah and Anna Shaw, who came from Abington, Mass., and settled here in 1792, on the homestead occupied by the late Freeman Shaw. Dr. Shaw was born in Abington, Mass., May 6, 1790, being less than two years old when his parents settled here. After attending for some time the school of Rev. Moses Hallock, he studied medicine with Dr. Peter Bryant of Cummington, father of Wm. Cullen Bryant. In 1819 and 1820 he attended medical lectures in Boston. He became Dr. Bryant's partner in practice, the partnership being continued until the death of the latter. In 1821 he married Dr. Bryant's daughter, Sarah Snell Bryant. He was licensed as a medical practitioner the same year. The following is a copy of his certificate:

{ L. }
{ S. }   COMMONWEALTH OF MASSACHUSETTS.

We the subscribers, Censors of the Massachusetts Medical Society, duly appointed and authorized, have examined Samuel Shaw of Cummington, in the County of Hampshire, a candidate for the Practice of Physick and Surgery; and having found him qualified, do appoint and license him as a Practitioner in Medicine, agreeable to the law in that case made and provided. Dated at Northampton, this 3rd day of May, A. D. one thousand eight hundred and twenty-one.

ELIHU DWIGHT,
WILLIAM HOOKER,
JOS. H. FLINT.

By virtue of the power in me vested, I have hereunto affixed the seal of the Massachusetts Medical Society.

JOS. FISHER, M. D., *President.*

Attest,   JOHN DIXWELL, M. D., *Rec. Secretary.*

After Dr. Bryant's death, Dr. Shaw in 1824 removed to Plainfield and commenced practice. His wife deceased Dec. 12, 1824, of consumption. This sad event inspired the beautiful poem of her distinguished brother, Wm. C. Bryant, entitled "The Death of the Flowers." In 1830 Dr. Shaw married Elizabeth Owen Clarke of Northamp-

Samuel Shaw
AT 60.

ton, daughter of Joseph Clarke, a lawyer descended from the Cooks, Lymans, Pomeroys, and other early settlers of that town, and the adopted son of Major Joseph Hawley. Elizabeth's beauty, grace and lovely character, were the theme of many a letter written by old Dr. Flint of Northampton to Dr. Shaw, before the engagement. She died Sept. 27, 1863. Dr. Shaw at first lived in the house lately re-modeled by Wm. Winslow. In 1833 he built the house which he occupied during the remainder of his life, and which is still owned by his daughters, who occupy it during the summer and fall months. It was thoroughly built and is now in an excellent state of preservation. Dr. Shaw was in active practice until 1854. In the fall of that year he was called one evening to attend his married daughter then living in West Cummington. While descending the hill in the southwest part of the town, some portion of the carriage suddenly gave way, and he was thrown violently to the ground. Being a large, heavy man, the shock was a very severe one, from which he never fully recovered. He was able however to occasionally visit patients for some years after, but always with some one to drive his horse. The writer remembers him as one who always had a good story to tell and liked a joke. His jolly " Haw, haw, haw," rings in my ears yet. One little episode I will relate. A near neighbor had several large boys who were inclined to be unruly. The neighbor was a rather quick tempered man, and one morning, one of his boys having provoked him in some way, he gave him a sounding box on the ear, the doctor being an unseen witness. The boy moaned greatly, and carried his head to one side, pretending that he could not lift it to its normal position. The doctor watching the boy occasionally through the day from his office window, noticed that when his father was out of sight, his head resumed its natural position. If his father appeared, his neck was at once bent as before. Toward evening, the father becoming somewhat alarmed, visited the doctor in company with his son, whose head still hung on one side. "Doctor," said he, "I am a little hasty, and when I gave the boy a cuff this morning, I suppose I gave him a harder blow than I intended, and he don't seem to be able to straighten his neck since. Now what treatment would you advise?" "Well," said the doctor, deliberately, drawing down the corners of his eye brows, "In my opinion, the best thing you can do, would be to hit him a *thundering* crack on the other ear." The boy did not wait to have his father follow this advice, but at once made off with head erect.—The doctor was tenderly cared for in his declining years by his daughters. He deceased Sept. 24, 1870, aged 80. He was for many years prominent in town affairs, being for eight years one of the selectmen. His office has been preserved in very much the same condition in which he left it. The case of books and the iron mortar and pestle used in compounding medicines, once belonged to Dr. Peter Bryant, and were used by him, previous to their coming into Dr. Shaw's possession. He was for forty years a member of the Mass. Medical Society. His quick intuitions and great skill, combined with a keen knowledge of human nature and a cheerful disposition, made him a successful and popular physician.

LATER PRACTITIONERS.

Dr. Chas. Bowker came here about 1855, but remained only a year or two. Dr. J. M. Eaton settled here about 1858, and remained two or three years. Dr. G. H. Taylor came here about 1863, and practiced until his death in 1873, except one year, when he was absent in the army. Dr. O. H. Lamb practiced here a few months about 1874. Dr. Daniel E. Thayer commenced practice here in 1875, and remained here two or three years. Dr. G. R. Fessenden came here in 1879, and remained about a year, when he removed to Ashfield. He is now often called to visit patients here. Since his removal we have had no resident physician.

JUSTICES OF THE PEACE.

So far as known, the first Justice in town was James Richards, who was commissioned June 8, 1802. Others were commissioned in the order named. Ebenezer Colson, Cyrus Joy, Iram Packard, Elijah Warner, Sr., John Mack, Sr., Erastus Bates, Leavitt Hallock, Jason Richards, Elijah Clark, Isaac K. Lincoln, George Vining, David Shaw, Wm. Gurney, Albert Dyer, Fred E. Campbell, James A. Winslow, Charles N. Dyer. L. Campbell was appointed a Notary Public in 1887.

CHAPTER X.

REVOLUTIONARY PENSIONERS.—SOLDIERS OF 1812.—ARTILLERY COMPANY.—LIST OF SOLDIERS IN WAR OF THE REBELLION.—DEATHS AMONG.—G. A. R. POST.

The following list of Revolutionary Pensioners, we copy from Dr. Porter's history of Plainfield. It contains the names of those still living in 1833, with the amount drawn annually by each. The amount is believed to have been based on their length of service.

Lemuel Allis,	$ 96	Rev. Moses Hallock,	$ 23$\frac{33}{100}$
Joseph Barnard,	96	Jacob Nash,	100
Ebenezer Bisbee,	20	Phillip Packard,	96
John Campbell,	23$\frac{33}{100}$	Whitcomb Pratt,	80
Vinson Curtis,	80	James Richards,	25$\frac{55}{100}$
Ebenezer Dickinson,	30	Josiah Shaw,	80
James Dyer,	100	Samuel Streeter,	96
Joseph Gloyd,	20	Josiah Torrey,	106$\frac{66}{100}$

Caleb White, 32$\frac{33}{100}$

At least two of our citizens served in the war of 1812. These were Orrin Tirrell and Samuel Thayer, Jr. It is believed that they were not called out of the state, but did military duty in the vicinity of Boston for a few weeks.

There was another who though not a citizen of the town at the time of the war, settled here immediately afterwards—Lieut. Brackley Shaw, who lived on the farm afterwards occupied by the late Jared Dyer. During the war of 1812 Lieut. Shaw had command of a battery on an island in Boston harbor. In 1825 he removed to Ira, N. Y., and ten years later to Michigan, being one of the pioneer settlers of that state. His son, Brackley Shaw, Jr., had in 1887 been for 14 years a member of the Michigan legislature, serving six years as senator. Another son, Rev. Horatio Watson Shaw, went to India in 1850, to take charge of the Mission College at Allahabad, returning after six years service.

THE ARTILLERY COMPANY.

This company was first organized in Williamsburg, and from thence, as it drew many of its recruits from the hill towns, the company armory and guns were successively removed to Goshen, and in the early part of the present century to Plainfield. One of the early Captains of the Company after its headquarters were established here, was Noah Joy of Hawley, who was afterward Colonel of the 3rd Artillery Regiment, of which perhaps this company may have been the nucleus. About 1820 the musicians of the company were Levi Campbell and Wm. Wilcutt, Sr., fifers, and Oliver Pool, drummer. In those days the State Militia was not fostered and petted by Government as at present, but each soldier must arm, equip and uniform himself, lose his time while on duty and pay his own expenses. So few there were who felt equal to the sacrifice that recruits were drawn from eight different towns, viz. : Plainfield, Goshen, Chesterfield, Savoy, Windsor, Cummington, Hawley and Ashfield. Among the first captains of the company were Capt. Eldridge, Levi Cook, Wm. Joy, Harry Torrey,* David R. Whiting,* Randall Dyer, John Mack,* Charles W. Parker and James Cook; later, Leonard Campbell* and Levi N. Campbell, all citizens of

Plainfield. Those of the above marked with a star after name, were honored later by being elected field officers in the 3rd Artillery Regiment. Levi N. Campbell was by the unanimous vote of the Regiment elected Major, but declined. While he was captain, in 1847, the state authorities, at his request, granted an order for building a new armory, the old one which stood near the present site of J. N. Benjamin's house, having become unfit for use. The contract was given to the late David Shaw, who erected the building a few rods east of where Jeremiah Tyrrell lives, and finished it to the acceptance of the Adjutant General. It was used as an armory until the company and regiment disbanded. As late as 1860 it was sold, removed to the upper village, re-modeled into a dwelling, and is now owned and occupied by Mrs. Frances P. Clark (since deceased). About the time the new armory was built, the state supplied the regiment with the old Springfield musket and required the rank and file to drill with them, and to practice the manual of arms; but the project was only a partial success, the soldiers not taking kindly to the clumsy arm, and they were soon called in. About this time the old four pounder brass cannon were exchanged for new six pounders. L. N. Campbell having resigned, he was succeeded as captain by Edward Bridgman of Goshen, and he by Levi Gardner of Ashfield. Among the Lieutenants of the company were Madison Knowlton of Ashfield, Henry Joy of Hawley, Abishur Nash, Daniel Stockwell, Philander Packard, Thomas Packard and Ansel K. Bradford of Plainfield. Bradford was afterwards chosen captain, and held that office when the company disbanded. Among those who served as musicians, were L. N. Campbell, William and Abner Gurney, Orson S. White, Lyman

K. Thayer, Leonard and J. Lyman Campbell, Milleon S. Colburn, Sylvanus Rice, Isaiah Stetson, Orrin Stetson, Isaac S. Nash, Calvin Shaw and Horace Hamlen. The late Apollos Gardner belonged to this company, and will be well remembered by those members still living. He used to "thumb the piece." The cannon by continuous firing soon became heated and I suppose the merest spark sometimes remained in the breech. It was his duty to hold his thumb over the touch-hole while the gun was being re-loaded. As soon as he removed it, the draft of air thus admitted fanned the latent spark within, and a discharge immediately followed. A cot of deerskin was usually worn on the thumb for protection, but he was sometimes without this. He never flinched, though his thumb was sometimes badly burned, and never permitted a premature discharge. Among the members of the company Capt. Ansel K. Bradford, Isaac S. Nash and Chas. S. Stetson served in the civil war, and probably a number of others.

SOLDIERS IN WAR OF THE REBELLION.

Plainfield furnished during this war sixty-one men, an excess of seven over all calls. The following is a list, the names occurring in the order of their enlistment, together with the regiment and company in which they served, also date of mustering in and of discharge or death. Mass. Infantry is understood, and their rank as private, unless otherwise stated.

	Co. and Reg't.		Mustered In.	Discharged.
Chauncey C. Shaw,	H	27	Sept. 20, '61.	Mar. 31, '63.
Wesley Woodard, Corp.	C	"	Oct. 1, "	Oct. — '62.
Newell Dyer, 2d.,	C	31	" 12, "	Apr. 11, "
do. 2d enlistment,	C	12	Sept. 12, '63.	Dec. 12, '63.

84   HISTORY OF PLAINFIELD.

	Co. and Reg't.		Mustered In.	Discharged.
Henry Y. Town,	C 4 N.Y.Ind.Bat.		Oct. 18, '61.	Oct. 17, '64.
Sherlock H. Lincoln,	E	1 Cav.	Dec. 9, "	Nov. 14, '62.
Hosea L. Thayer,	E	"	" 16, "	July 21, '65.
H. Dwight Gloyd,	C	31	Feb. 1, '62.	Jan. 31, "
Wm. A. Hallock,	K	23	Aug. 4, "	
do. 2d enlistment,	"	"	Dec. 1, '63.	July 20, '65.
Lorenzo Streeter, Corp.	H	37	Aug. 15,'62.	Nov. 21, '63.
Nelson W. Cook,	"	"	" " "	Aug. 14, "
Almon M. Warner, Lt.,	"	"	" " "	Aug. 28, '65.
Fordyce A. Dyer, 2d Lt.	F	46	Sept. 26, "	
do. 2d enlist'nt, 1st	" F 2 H.Art.		'63. d.	Oct.26,'64.
Franklin Cook,	F	46	Sept.26,62. d.	June 20,'63.
Newcomb Dyer,	"	"	" " "	July 29, "
Chas. C. Gloyd,	"	"	" " "	
do. 2d enlistment,	A 2 H.Art.		May 27, '63.	Sept. 3, '65.
J. Wesley Gurney,	F	46	Sept. 26, '62.	
do. 2d enlistment,	— 2 H.Art.		June 5, '63.	Dec. 30, '63.
Stephen Hayward,Jr.Corp.	F 46		Sept. 26,'62.	July 29, "
Samuel W. Jones,	F	46	" " "	" " "
Robert P. Loud,	"	"	" " "	
do. 2d enlistment,	A 2 H.Art.		May 28, '63.	Sept. 3, '65.
Chas. S. Stetson,	F	46	Sept.26,'62.	July 29, '63.
Geo. W. King,	"	"	" " "	" " "
Clifford Packard, Corp.,	"	"	" " "	" " "
Josiah Rood,	"	"	" " " d. "	10, "
Theodore W. Shaw,	"	"	" " "	" 29, "
Allen Smith,	"	"	" " "	
do. 2d enlistment,	—2 H.Art.		June 5, '63.	Sept. 3, '65.
Wm. Edwards Warner,	F	46	Sept.26,62.	d.June 28,63.
Alden H. Dyer,	"	"	" " "	d. Jan. 19, "
Ira W. Hamlen, Corp.,	"	"	" " "	July 29, "

SOLDIERS IN WAR OF THE REBELLION. 85

	Co. and Reg't.	Mustered in.	Discharged.
Justus W. Gurney,	F 46	Sept. 26,'62.	
do. 2d enlistment,	— 2 H. Art.	June 5, '63.	Deserted.
Oliver C. Burr,	E 46	Oct. 15,'62.	July 29,'63.
Wm. W. Vanalstine,	— 2 H. Art.	Dec. 7, '63.	Died — —
Wm. J. Nash,	D 34	Mch. 1, '64.	June 19,'65.
John C. Dean,	F 2 H. Art.	Aug. 25, "	" 26, "
Arthur W. Robinson,	" " "	" " "	" " "
Winthrop B. Robinson,	" " "	" " "	" " "
Wm. L. Lucas,	" " "	" " "	" " "
John Stewart,	" " "	" " "	" " "
G. H. Taylor, Hos. Stew.	" " "	Sept. 1,	" May 23, "

The following persons were drafted and obtained substitutes. 1863, Nathan Barton, Joseph O. Gloyd, Nahum S. Packard, Horatio A. Shaw, James A. Winslow. 1864, Stillman F. Dyer, Levi W. Gloyd.

The following persons were drafted in 1863, and rejected. Henry W. Beals, Chas. C. Clark, Ansel B. Cole, Newell Dyer, 2d, Jeremiah T. Gardner, Geo. Richards, Thaddeus Rood, Sylvester Stetson.

The following are the names of substitutes furnished:

Alfred Videtto.	Thaddeus Connors, Springfield.
Morris Bishop.	Thos. Figges, Boston.
Danford Glazier.	Arthur Hitchcock, Charlemont.
Milo Lucas.	James Stanard, Guilford, Vt.
	Peter Taylor.

The following Plainfield men were in the service but were credited to some other town:

	Co. and Reg't.	Mustered In.	Discharged.
Isaac S. Nash,	D 34	July 31,'62.	June 16, '65.
Charles Gurney,	E 37	Sept. 2,	" k'd. July 2,'63.
Edw. F. Hamlen, Sergt.	I 52	Oct. 11,	" Aug. 14. "

	Co. and Reg't.	Mustered In.	Discharged.
Almorin S. Latham,	D 49	Sept. 19, "	Sept. 1, 63.
Sidney H. Latham,	" "	" " "	" " "
James Wetherbee,	C 10	June 21,'61,	Dec. 21, "
Harrison Loud,	I 57	Mch. 10,'64, d.	Aug. 1,'64.

The following now residing here, served to credit of other towns, as given below :

Geo. W. Billings, Monson, E 10; June 21, '61; July 1, '64.
Edwin A. Atkins, Sergt. 1 Conn. Cav.; Dec. 9,'61; Dec.—'64.
Wm. H. Packard, Windsor, I 49; Nov. 19, '62; Sept. 1,'63.
Shepard R. Dyer, Corp., Conway, C 31; Nov. 20, '61; Sept. 9, '65.
Onslow Taylor, Corp., Hawley, I 52; Oct. 11, '62; Aug. 14, '63.
Melvin Packard, Northampton, D 34; Jan. 4,'64; Jan. 20,'66.
Leander J. Beals, Huntington, H. 37; Aug. 30, '62; April 27, '63.
Melville C. Butler, Buckland, K 60; July 22, '64; Dec. 3, '64.
James W. Loud, F 22 Iowa; Aug. 14, '62; June 14, '65.
Norman W. Stetson, Cheshire, I 49; Sept. 19, 62; Sept. 1,'63.

Sept. 26, 1862, 18 men from Plainfield were mustered in, it being by far the largest number who enlisted at any one time. These were all members of Co. F 46 Mass. Only one man was killed while in service, Charles Gurney, son of Wm. Gurney, at Gettysburg, July 2, 1863. Six died from disease, viz.: Alden H. Dyer, son of Samuel Dyer, at Newbern, N. C., of typhoid fever, Jan. 19, 1863. His remains were brought to Plainfield for interment.—Franklin Cook, son of James Cook, died at Beaufort, N. C., June 20, 1863.—Wm. Edwards Warner, son of Wm. Warner, died at Newbern, N. C., June 28, 1863, of typhoid fever.—Josiah Rood died on shipboard, 24 hours out of

Boston harbor, July 10, 1863, of consumption. and exhaustion caused by sea-sickness. He was in poor health most of the time while in the army and was unable to do regular duty. His courage was good, however, and he embarked at Newbern, feeling that when he reached home his health would improve, but his strength gave out and he died as above stated. His body was brought home for interment.—Lieut. Fordyce A. Dyer, son of Albert Dyer, died at Newbern, N. C., of yellow fever, Oct. 26, 1864. He was detailed as City Inspector during the prevalence of the yellow fever and fell a victim of this terrible disease. His remains were subsequently brought home for interment.— H. Harrison Loud, son of James Loud, died Aug. 1, 1864, of typhoid dysentery, at Chestnut Hill hospital, Philadelphia, and was brought home for burial.— Wm. W. Vanalstine (colored) is reported as dying in the service, but the Adjutant General's rolls give no particulars.

PENSIONERS.

The following named veterans, now residing here, are in receipt of pensions:

Edwin A. Atkins, $4 per mo.   Wm. H. Packard, $6 per mo.
Leander J. Beals, $8 " "   Melvin Packard, $10 " "
Nelson W. Cook, $8 " "   Onslow Taylor, $12 " "
   Norman W. Stetson, $8 per mo.

Mrs. Mary A. Dunning, widowed mother of Samuel J. Dunning, draws a pension of $12 per month, and Mrs. Susan E. Taylor, widow of Dr. G. H. Taylor, $8 per month.

G. A. R. POST.

Mountain Miller Post No. 198, G. A. R., was organized here in 1889. It consists of 22 members. The officers for 1891 are as follows:

Commander, E. A. Atkins.
Senior Vice Com., Onslow Taylor.
Junior " " Geo. W. King.
Adjutant, Nelson W. Cook.
Quartermaster, J. W. Loud.
Chaplain, A. N. Hubbard, Windsor.
Officer of the Day, Shepard R. Dyer.
" " Guard, L. J. Beals.
Sergeant Major, Geo. W. Billings.
Q. M. Sergeant, Wells P. Taylor, Ashfield.
Surgeon, M. C. Butler.
Color Bearers, { John Campbell, Savoy. Norman W. Stetson.

It is believed that this post covers the largest area of any in the state, it having members from seven different towns and three counties. Capt. Edward F. Hamlen, chief clerk of the Executive Department of the State, who resides here a portion of the summer, is a member of this Post.

CHAPTER XI.

COLLEGE GRADUATES AND PROFESSIONAL MEN.

[The writer is indebted to an article in the Hampshire County Gazetteer from the pen of the Rev. Solomon Clark, for much of the material for this chapter.]

LAWYERS.

Cyrus Joy, son of Jacob, graduated at Williams College in 1811. Studied law and practiced in Northampton, afterwards in this town. Removed to Philadelphia, where he deceased a few years since.

Hosea F. Stockwell, lived forty years at the West, having an extensive practice in New Philadelphia, O.

Elisha Bassett, son of Thomas, for half a century connected with the U. S. District Court at Boston.

Alden B. Vining graduated at Williams College in 1843. Located in Bridgeport, Conn. Died in New Haven.

Erastus N. Bates graduated at Williams College in 1853, studied law, but his health did not allow him to pursue its practice. Has been twice, at least, State Treasurer of Illinois.

E. Livingstone Lincoln, son of Isaac K., graduated at Willams College in 1853. Admitted to the bar in 1858. Died in Westfield, Mass., in 1859.

Almon M. Warner, son of James, is now in practice at Cincinnati, O.

CHAS. DUDLEY WARNER.

HIS BIRTHPLACE.

EDITORS, PROFESSORS AND TEACHERS.

EDITORS AND LITERARY PERSONS.

Gerard Hallock (see genealogical history of Hallock family.)

Charles Dudley Warner, son of Justus Warner, was born Sept. 12, 1829, on the homestead where the late Francis W. Joy lived, a mile north of the village. He graduated at Hamilton College in 1851. Is well known as an author and is one of the editors of the Hartford Courant. The engraving of his birthplace is from a photograph, and shows it as it now appears.

Mrs. Fidelia Cook, daughter of Stephen Hayward, for some time superintended the literary department of the Springfield Republican.

Mrs. Martha J. Lamb (see genealogical history of Jacob Nash family.)

PROFESSORS AND TEACHERS.

James Hayward, Jr., graduated at Harvard in 1819. Was tutor there. Afterwards professor of mathematics and natural philosophy. Published "Elements of Geometry."

Isaac Newton Lincoln graduated at Williams in 1847. Was professor of Latin and French at that college for nine years. Died in 1862.

Tilly Brown Hayward, son of Capt. James, born April 2, 1797. Graduated at Harvard in 1820. Was for many years a teacher. Later a preacher in the Swedenborgian denomination.

Alden Porter Beals, son of Dea. Robert, graduated at Williams in 1849. High school teacher for more than 30 years, much of the time at Stamford, Conn., where he deceased a few years since.

Francis Torrey, superintendent of schools in Newark, N. J., (see genealogical history of Josiah Torrey family.)

Charles Lyman Shaw, son of Dr. Samuel, graduated at Williams in 1864. Has for many years taught a classical school at Astoria, N. Y.

PHYSICIANS.

Dr. Samuel Shaw. (See Chap. IX.)

Dana Shaw. (See genealogical history of Josiah Shaw family.)

Washington Shaw, nephew of above. Settled in Williamsburg, Mass.

Joseph Richards, a brother of the missionaries, long a physician in Hillsdale, N. Y.

Chilion Packard, in early life went South.

Seth H. Pratt, went West many years ago.

Newell White, still living in Pennsylvania.

Royal Joy, studied with Dr. Samuel Shaw and settled in Cummington.

Francis Pratt, a practicing physician in Ohio.

Newton Robinson, also a physician in the same state.

James F. Richards, son of Jason, a physician in Andover, Mass.

Lewis Whiting, deceased a few years since in Saratoga, N. Y.

J. Emerson Warner, son of James, now practicing in Sterling, Va.

Daniel E. Thayer, a physician at Adams, Mass.

Dr. Shepard L. Hamlen was a dentist in Cincinnati, O.

Dr. Joseph Beals, a long time dentist in Greenfield, Mass.

Geo. Burt, a dentist in Springfield, Mass.

Samuel Francis Shaw, son of Dr. Samuel, was born at

Plainfield, Sept. 7, 1833. He was fitted for college at the Northampton Collegiate Institute. Entered Williams College in 1852, and was graduated in 1855. After graduation he remained at home four years, studying medicine with his father and making collections of native plants and birds. He studied medicine at the College of Physicians and Surgeons in New York, graduating in 1862. A few months later he entered the navy as assistant surgeon. During his service of nineteen years he made many long voyages, visiting the West Indies, the Azores, Peru, Sitka, China, Japan and Siberia. He married Oct. 27, 1877, Adelaide Roberts, daughter of Edward Roberts, Esq., of Philadelphia, and sister of the well-known artist, Howard Roberts, whose statue of Fulton is in the Capitol at Washington. After spending a year with his wife in traveling through Europe, he resigned his surgeon's commission and settled in Philadelphia. He died at his home 1909 Walnut St., Dec. 7, 1884. Dr. Shaw was a man of commanding presence. His tall and well proportioned figure, over six feet in height, together with a handsome face which was lighted up by a pair of blue eyes of unusual softness and beauty, attracted universal attention. While his great dignity of character inspired respect, his unselfishness won the affection of all who knew him.

Dr. Marcus Whitman, noted as a missionary, physician and surgeon for more than ten years in Oregon, also for the long, tedious journey which he made across the Rocky Mountains in mid-winter to Washington, D. C., when Daniel Webster was Secretary of State, spent many of his boyhood days in Plainfield, living until early manhood with Col. John Packard, whose home was the same now occupied by Albert N. Gurney. He attended the school of Rev. Moses Hallock, which perhaps had much to do with shaping his subsequent career. Having graduated at the Pittsfield medical school, he became in 1835 a missionary of the American Board. The next year in company with Rev. H. H. Spaulding, they with their wives crossed the Rocky Mountains and located in Oregon. Visiting as surgeon the various forts of the Hudson Bay Co., Dr. Whitman became convinced that the plan of that company was to secure that vast territory with all its wealth and resources for Great Britain. To make the story brief, he started to cross the continent in mid-winter, reaching Missouri in February, 1843, frost bitten and exhausted. Here he engaged to pilot a colony in the spring to the Columbia River, contradicting the reports that wagons could *not* cross the mountains. Hurrying on to Washington he called on Daniel Webster, then Secretary of State, and also on President Tyler, affirming that wagons and emigrants could cross the mountains, which they were loth to believe. Webster said, "I am about trading that *worthless* territory for some valuable concessions in relation to the Newfoundland cod-fisheries." Dr. Whitman replied with earnestness, "I hope you will not do it, sir. We want that *valuable* territory ourselves." The president finally said : "Dr. Whitman, since you are a missionary, I will believe you, and if you take your emigrants over there on your return, as you propose, the treaty will not be ratified" In March he was back in Missouri and led a thousand emigrants to Fort Hall. Here the commander of the fort, in the service of the Hudson Bay Co., offered to give them pack horses in exchange for their wagons, declaring that they could not cross the mountains with them. This offer was refused, and after a long but successful journey, he and his 800 emigrants, with their wagons, emerged on the plains of the Columbia River Sept. 4, 1843. The treaty was not signed. Oregon and the Northern Pacific coast were saved to the United States by the heroism, energy and zeal of this noble man.

MINISTERS.

Jephthah Pool, many years ago a pastor in Windsor, Mass.

James and William Richards, foreign missionaries. (See genealogical history of James Richards family.)

Wm. A. Hallock. (See Hallock family.)

Erastus Dickinson, son of Ebenezer, born April 1, 1807. Graduated at Amherst, 1832.

Austin Richards, D. D., brother of the missionaries.

David Rood, born in Buckland, Mass., April 25, 1818. Removed with his parents to Plainfield in 1824. Graduated at Williams College in 1844, and at what is now Hartford theological seminary in 1847. Married Miss A. V. Pixley, sister of Stephen Pixley, Oct. 3, 1847, was ordained, and they sailed for Natal, So. Africa, the same month, as missionaries of the American Board to the Zulus. In 1860 they visited the old home, and in 1888, after 40 years of faithful service, they returned to the United States and settled at Covert, Mich., near Mr. Rood's brothers. He deceased from a paralytic shock, April 8, 1891. His name will stand and endure with the names of Moffat and Livingstone. "Blessed are the dead which die in the Lord, from henceforth. Yea, saith the Spirit, that they may rest from their labors; and their works do follow them."

Stephen C. Pixley, born June 23, 1829. Educated for the ministry. Graduated at Williams in 1852, and at East

Windsor Hill (Conn.) Theological Seminary in 1855. Married Louisa Healy of Chesterfield in 1855. Was ordained at Plainfield the same year, and entered the service of the American Board as a missionary. His field of labor was among the Zulus with David Rood, with which mission he is still connected. He visited the United States and his old home a few years since.

Isaac Newton Lincoln, before mentioned, professor in Williams College.

Spencer O. Dyer, minister in the Methodist denomination.

James Clark and Thomas Thayer, both ministers in the Baptist denomination.

William A. Hallock, 2d, and Leavitt H. Hallock. (See Hallock family.)

Rev. Solomon Clark, a native of Northampton, born March 2, 1811. Pastor of the Plainfield church and closely identified with the interests of the people for over 28 years. He came here from Canton, Mass., in Jan. 1858. Married for his second wife, Mrs. Lucy E. Gilbert, widow of W. C. Gilbert, Oct. 5, 1858. They have one daughter, Elizabeth Richards, born Oct. 5, 1859. Married Wm. H. Gardiner, July 26, 1880. Now reside in Chicago. Mr. Clark in addition to his pastoral duties, has written and published a history of Northampton and its old families, in which line he particularly excels. It is considered a valuable work. He is now engaged in preparing a history of the First Church in Northampton, and its members.

DAVID SHAW.

Although he was not a professional man, the author feels that this work would be incomplete without at least a brief mention. He was the son of Nehemiah Shaw,

DAVID SHAW.

was born June 15, 1794, being the oldest of a family of sixteen children. His parents lived in a house which stood opposite the north cemetery on lot now owned by J. N. Benjamin. His opportunities for obtaining an education were exceedingly limited. He attended school very little, if any, but nevertheless managed to obtain a much better than ordinary education. Was well versed in the higher branches of arithmetic and in his calculations used no rules laid down in the text books, but worked after rules of his own devising. Was an excellent and accurate surveyor. He was in the strictest sense a self-educated man. Possessed of great mechanical skill, he invented several useful instruments, which displayed great nicety of workmanship, among them a seed-sower and an odometer, an instrument to be attatched to a wheel for measuring distances. He married Elizabeth Randall, and lived for a time in Cummington, but returned to Plainfield, and in 1842 built the house just west of the meeting-house, since occupied by himself and his son Horatio. His principal business for many years, particularly toward the latter part of his life, was repairing watches and clocks, in which business he had a great local reputation. Until a few months before his death, his form was as erect, his eye as bright, his step as nimble, and his hand as steady as a man of forty. He deceased Oct. 6, 1884, in his 91st year.

J. T. KIRKLAND HAYWARD.

Son of Stephen Hayward. Left town when a young man. Became interested in railroads. At the time of the late civil war was president of the Hannibal & St. Joseph Mo. railroad. The people of Missouri were quite evenly divided in sentiment between the Union and rebel cause.

Mr. Hayward was a strong Union man, and rendered substantial aid to the cause. On this account, as well as a preparatory step toward gaining possession of the H. & St. Jo. R. R., several prominent rebels made an attempt to kidnap him. They took him into custody one night, and all entered an empty box-car. Mr. Hayward, who had not been bound, managed in some way to slip out of the door, which he slammed together and locked, thus completely turning the tables on his would-be captors. They were of course unable to escape. Mr. Hayward at once ordered an engine to be attached to the car, and it was with its inmates taken to the eastern part of the state, where they were delivered up to the Federal authorities.

CHAPTER XII.

CENSUS.—VALUATION.--LIST OF VOTERS.—POLITICAL PARTIES.—CAMPAIGN OF 1840. BITS FROM THE OLD RECORDS.--INCIDENTS AND REMINISCENCES.--FIRES.

The following figures show the population of the town for the last hundred years:

1790—458.	1840—910.	1870—521.
1800—797.	1850—814.	1875—481.
1810—977.	1855—652.	1880—457.
1820—936.	1860—639.	1885—453.
1830—984.	1865—579.	1890—436.

The deaths in the last decade outnumber the births by 37. This shows that 16 more have moved into town than have removed from town in that time. The writer is of the opinion that the population has reached its lowest figures and that the next census will show an increase from the last.

The following is from the Assessors' books for 1890:

No. of residents assessed on property,	106
" " non-residents " " "	51
" " Polls "	147
Assessed value of personal estate,	$ 37,880
" " " land,	76,000
" " " buildings,	38,525
Total assessed valuation,	$152,405
Tax rate per $1,000,	$16

HISTORY OF PLAINFIELD.

Acres of land assessed, 12,795
No. of dwelling-houses, 116
No. of horses, 148—Cows, 440—Sheep, 396—Neat cattle other than cows, 302—Swine, 123.

LIST OF VOTERS, MARCH 2, 1891.

	Age.		Age.
Atkins, Edwin A.	58	Cook, Nelson W.	50
Benjamin, James N.	51	Cook, Homer	59
Barton, Henry S.	66	Clark, Levi	88
Barton, Nathan	55	Clark, Chas. C.	54
Barton, Geo. N.	27	Clark, Seth W.	57
Burt, Sumner	75	Clark, Fred D.	31
Burt, Edmund	35	Clark, Henry D.	25
Burt, Chas. R.	45	Colburn, Millson S.	83
Burt, Orsamus C.	21	Cleveland, Wm. M.	72
Barker, Isaac T.	82	Cudworth, Paul H.	68
Beals, H. Harrison	50	Cudworth, Frank B.	34
Beals, Henry W.		Dunham, Warren I.	49
Beals, Fred W.	28	Dunham, Chas. F.	32
Beals, Leander J.	57	Dyer, Wm. H.	64
Blanchard, Oliver	56	Dyer, Chas. N.	41
Blanchard, Geo. A.		Dyer, Shepard R.	50
Bogart, Mandeville	56	Dyer, Elwin F.	38
Bogart, John	29	Gardner, Apollos H.	61
Billings, Geo. W.	48	Gardner, Jason W.	60
Butler, Melville C.	54	Gardner, Jeremiah T.	58
Campbell, Leonard	79	Gardner, Ira J.	27
Cole, Ansel B.	57	Gardner, Nelson W.	25
Cole, Arthur T.	30	Gardner, Eugene H.	30
Cole, Fred S.	21	Gloyd, Bethuel	81
Cook, John F.	55	Gloyd, Levi W.	57

LIST OF VOTERS, MARCH 2, 1891.

	Age.		Age.
Gloyd, Joseph O.	49	Packard, H. Clark	50
Gloyd, Edwin S.	21	Packard, Harold S.	30
Griggs, Amos K.	73	Packard, Henry C.	24
Gurney, James F.	45	Packard, Cyrus W.	38
Gurney, Albert N.	43	Packard, B. Franklin	32
Gould, Daniel H.	51	Parker, Eugene L.	45
Gould, Clark F.	25	Parsons, Stephen	50
Harris, Geo. E.	50	Richmond, Austin L.	61
Harris, Daniel	52	Richmond, Albert F.	22
Harris, James P.	28	Rice, Frederic M.	26
Holden, Chas. N.	43	Sears, Joseph W.	39
Holden, Frank A.	34	Sears, Samuel H.	36
Howes, Mark E.	40	Shaw, Horatio A.	69
Ingraham, Frank C.	28	Shaw, Willie E.	34
Jones, William	58	Streeter, Lester E.	39
Joy, Lorenzo W.	58	Streeter, Alden E.	29
King, Geo. W.	58	Starks, Wilbur J.	27
Kinney, Edwin R.	67	Stetson, Marshall	47
Kinney, Theron E.	38	Stetson, Nelson B.	25
Loud, James W.	56	Stetson, Orren M.	23
Mason, Ira	76	Stetson, Sylvester R.	59
Mason, Thos. G.		Smith, Clark	66
Mason, Lemuel	51	Taylor, Onslow	52
Mason, Ezra H.	45	Taylor, Henry E.	26
Mason, Edward W.	33	Taylor, Frank G.	31
McCloud, Edward I.	29	Thatcher, Eugene	33
Nash, James A.	53	Thayer, Fred T.	32
Packard, David	71	Thayer, Lester D.	28
Packard, Sylvester	65	Thayer, Lyman K.	79
Packard, Wm. H.	68	Thayer, Frank L.	46
Packard, Luther W.	35	Thayer, Amasa W.	

Thayer, Samuel B.	74	White, Lucian A.	39
Tirrell, Almon B.	31	Whiting, Wm. C.	77
Tirrell, Russell	76	Wheeler, Thos. K.	78
Tirrell, Arthur R.	37	Wheeler, Norman	32
Tirrell, Orren	68	Willcutt, William	55
Tyrrell, Jeremiah J.	82	Willcutt, Geo. L,	33
Torrey, Merritt	65	Willcutt, Horace	63
Torrey, Alden L.	30	Winslow, William	78
Torrey, Edwin T.	69	Winslow, James A.	51
Torrey, Geo. A.	30		

Whole number, 131.

The following persons are eligible, or soon will be, to register as voters, but have not done so : Chas. L. Alexander, Henri H. Fenton, Wm. H. Leete, Newton K. Lincoln, Eugene F. Parker, Clark W. Streeter, Lyndon Wheeler, Rev. John A. Woodhull.

POLITICAL PARTIES.

Plainfield, like most of the Western Hampshire towns, ever since the formation of the present prominent political parties, has been strongly Republican. At the last Presidential election, 94 Republican votes were cast, 15 Democratic and 3 Prohibition. Chas. C. Clark is the present chairman of the Republican town committee and Wm. M. Cleveland of the Democratic. The Prohibitionists as yet have no town organization. Probably at no time in the history of the town or of the nation has political excitement run so high as in the Presidential campaign of 1840, when Martin Van Buren and Richard M. Johnson, Wm. Henry Harrison and John Tyler were the opposing candidates for President and Vice President. Several mass meetings were held in Painfield that fall, at which speeches were made and songs sung in the interest of the favorite candidates, Harrison and Tyler. "Tippecanoe and Tyler too," "Log cabin and hard cider," were the war cries of the whigs. On one of these occasions, a wagon 30 feet in length, specially constructed for the purpose, containing 90 persons, and drawn by thirteen yoke of oxen, driven by Russell Tirrell and others, came down from "Hallockville." It required no little skill to engineer the cumberous and lengthy vehicle around the numerous curves, but it was safely done, in spite of many predictions to the contrary. The writer has in his possession a tattered banner which did service during that memorable campaign, bearing this inscription: "Plainfield Whigs, True to Liberty and the Constitution. Nov. 2 Tells the Story." On the reverse is inscribed "Martin and Dick, Hang up your fiddle. Tip and Tyler are coming." The vote of Plainfield that fall was as follows: For Harrison electors, 176; for Van Buren electors, 27.

BITS FROM THE OLD RECORDS.

March 16, 1789, "Voted that the log-house Ichabod Pool put up on Doct. Solomon Bond's land, be made use of for a pound for the District." An article was inserted in the warrant for annual town meeting for many years "To see if the town will allow horses and swine to *goe* at large the present year." It was usually voted that swine at least be allowed to go at large, if well yoked and ringed. April 3, 1797, it was voted to build a stone pound 30 ft. square, the height and thickness of the walls being specified, and that the contract be set up at vendue to the lowest bidder. Struck off to Oliver Robinson for $37. For some reason he failed to build it, and March 12, 1798, it was

"Voted to build a wooden pound, thirty feet square, in the same manner that Cummington pound is built. To be built of hemlock timber by the first of July." This was built and used until 1807. April 6, 1807, it was voted to repair the pound; then the vote was reconsidered, and a "committy," consisting of John Hamlen, Jacob Nash and Edward Curtis, was appointed to inspect the old pound and report whether it was worth repairing, and voted to adjourn "fourteen night," to await their decision. They reported it not worth repairing, so it was set up at vendue and struck off to Josiah Torrey for 80 cts. Then voted to build one of stone "on the north side of the road, about 40 rods west of Joel Carr's." This spot is a little northwest of Charles Dunham's, and part of the wall may still be seen. The south wall was to be 3½ feet thick, the others 3 feet, and to average six feet high. The contract was awarded to Timothy Packard for $39.

Aug. 20, 1789, "Voted that the District shall procure a Drum and fife for the use of the foot company of militia. Voted that Capt. John Cunningham shall purchase the above Drum and fife."

June 27, 1794, "Voted to make up the pay to the Soldiers that may turn out to stand Ready to march at a minute's warning for the Defence of their Country, Seven Dollars per month with what is allowed by the Continent, exclusive of the Dollar and 60 cents per month allowed for Cloathing and three Dollars Bounty, provided they are called upon to march."

Sept. 9, 1800, "Voted to make provision for the Training soldiers at the General muster at Northampton. Voted that Lt. Jacob Allen, Mr. Elijah Warner, and Mr. Abel Warner be a committee to procure provision for the company. Voted that there be 25 lbs. Cheese, 120 lbs. Wheat bread and 100 lbs. Mutton provided for said company. Voted to allow Mr. Abel Warner five shillings for conveying and taking care of said provision."

Oct. 15, 1798, " Voted that Elijah Warner be directed to collect flax sufficient to purchase the town stock of *led*."

It appears that the persons named below in this certificate had been concerned in "Shay's Rebellion."

" A List of the several persons belonging to Plainfield who took and subscribed the Oath of Allegiance before Samuel Mather, Esq., January, 1787, viz.:

Moses Curtis, Stephen Steth, Isaac Joy, Solomon Nash, Tobias Green, Salmon Fay. N. B. No arms were returned to me.   S. MATHER, *Justice Peace*."

April 2, 1798, " Voted to procure a half Bushel and peck measure. Voted that a set of Brass Weights be procured to four pounds."

April 7, 1794, "Voted that Samuel Streeter be Sexton the present year. Sd. Streeter is to Receive for his Trouble in taking care of the meeting-house, sweeping the Alleys once a month, and the Seats and Pews once in three months, Eight shillings."

INCIDENTS AND REMINISCENCES.

Not long after the erection of the meeting-house belfry, as some boys were playing around the meeting-house, one of them, Comfort Beals by name, threw up a stone which struck the cock which was placed on the summit of the spire as a weather vane and bent his tail feathers. His comrades told him that he would be put to death, which it is presumed he actually believed, unless he went up and straightened them. In this dilemma, he climbed up by the lightning rod as far as the bell, where he rested awhile, and then ascended to the vane. After restoring the tail to its proper position, he descended, without meeting with any accident. Years afterward, his son, Levi, when the old meeting-house was about to be torn down, "for and in consideration of the sum of fifty cents to him in hand paid," ascended to the vane from the bell deck in the same way, removed it, and brought it down in safety. This vane was placed on Wm. Robinson's barn, where it did service until a few years since.

In June, 1829, as Capt. Levi Cook was engaged in shoeing a yoke of oxen, one of the animals being fastened by a chain to a staple, in attempting to extricate himself, pulled out the staple, and in doing this threw the chain round the man's legs, the hook catching with what is known as a "log hitch." The ox then took the road, and ran for about half a mile, dragging the unfortunate man after him. He was finally stopped by a boy. The Captain retained his faculties sufficiently to raise himself up, throw off the chain, give the ox a Scotch blessing, and invite him to proceed to a locality which we will not now name, and then fainted. He was severely bruised, and if his body had not been somewhat protected by his leather apron which dragged under him, his injuries would have been much more severe. He recovered after a tedious confinement. The shop where he was at work was the one that stood in the upper part of the village, nearly opposite where J. W. Sears now lives. The ox was stopped near the site of the Bates house, midway between the village and A. B. Cole's. The writer remembers Capt. Cook as being somewhat peculiar, quite nervous and excitable, but withal a good neighbor and a kind-hearted man. He was for many years the village sexton, ringing the bell at noon and 9 P. M. as regular as the sun. He also had the care of the meeting-house and rung the bell for Sunday services. About the time of the dismission of Rev. D. B. Bradford, the church and parish were divided on the subject, some being in favor of his dismissal and others opposed. One Sunday noon, the Captain, who was a warm friend of Mr. Bradford, while in the entry ringing the bell for the afternoon service, became involved in a somewhat heated discussion on the subject with some of the bystanders, in which he claimed that Mr. Bradford had been mis-used. Just then Mr. Bradford entered the porch, and overhearing a little of the conversation, said, "Why, Captain, you're getting *excited* are you not?" "Excited?" replied the old man in his thin, high-keyed voice, "No! I aint *excited*, but I'm *mad* as the devil." The Captain was a descendant of Francis Cook, who came over in the Mayflower, the descent being traced as follows : Francis, Jacob, Francis, Robert, Nathaniel, Levi and Levi, Jr. He was born in Abington, Mass., Feb. 14, 1783. Died Dec. 19, 1868.

About the year 1859, as William Warner's barn was being "launched," being drawn by two lines of oxen, assisted by a company of men, with the intention of placing it on a new site, it suddenly, without any warning, fell in a promiscuous heap. Strange as it may appear, none of the men or oxen were injured.

FIRES.

The following is a list of fires that have occurred in town. Probably all are not included : Joseph Beals' house was burnt February, 1789. Early in 1819 the house of Benj. Gardner, Jr. and Warren Gardner. April 22, 1824, Ira Hamlen's house, including a hat manufactory. February, 1825, the woolen factory of Arnold & Nahum Streeter. Dec. 13, 1833, the house of Stallham Rice, with all its contents, the family being absent. Dr. Porter, writing in 1834, says: "Four school-houses have been destroyed by fire, the last on Dec. 3, 1833. Two of these were in the northeast district. There have also been burnt four mechanics' shops and a small distillery." March 28, 1835, the house of Bela Dyer, where John F. Cook's house now stands, was burned. Mrs. Dyer was frying doughnuts, and the fat taking fire, ignited flax which was spread overhead, the house being unfinished. The house and barn of Rev. A. H. Sweet, which stood where the house of the late Mrs. Frances P. Clark now stands, were burned one Sunday evening in August, 1858. It was set in the barn by his son, then a small boy, while playing with matches. Probably a hundred people were there within ten or fifteen minutes after the fire broke out, it being about five o'clock, and many were on their way to evening service, it being a time of special religious interest. Nearly everything was saved from the buildings, including doors and windows, and had any proper apparatus been at hand, the house could probably have been saved, as a large tank of water holding many barrels was near. There was no insurance.—Geo. Vining had a barn burned one summer night, said to have been struck by lightning. Later, about 1860, his house and another barn were burned at different times. Cause of fire unknown. Fully insured. Not far from this time, an unoccupied house in the north part of the town, known as the "Livermore" house, owned by Leonard Joy, was

FIRES. 109

burned. Mr. Joy had kindled a fire in the fire-place while making some repairs on the interior of the building, the weather being cold, and while absent at a neighbors on some errand, the house took fire and was consumed. Feb. 22, 1861, the house of S. H. Lincoln was burned; supposed to have taken from a defective chimney. Insured for $700. Considerable clothing and furniture were destroyed. Mr. Lincoln owned an old house on the opposite side of the road, which he repaired and occupied.—About twenty years since, the old house formerly occupied by the late Samuel Davison, caught fire from a burning brush heap. The house was unoccupied. Loss small.— Francis W. Joy's carpenter's shop was burned in the spring of 1863.—A few years later Thomas Wheeler's barn was struck by lightning and destroyed.—The woolen factory of S. C. Streeter was burned in 1876. The loss of contents was nearly total. No insurance.—Ezra Tyrrell's house, occupied by Levi Blanchard, was burned in 1880. Supposed to have taken fire from a defective flue.—April 4, 1886, the house of Roswell Davison was burned. The chimney took fire in the morning and burned out, and being watched through the day was supposed to be all safe, though still hot at evening. During the night the fire broke out, and the house was consumed with most of its contents. Mr. Davison was quite ill at the time and unable to render much assistance. It was nearly burned down before any help arrived. Mrs. Davison and her daughter carried out some articles, but most of the clothing and bedding removed caught fire and were burned. Insurance $400.—March 12, 1889, the barns and carriage-house of Clark Smith, occupied by his son, Wm. C. Smith, took fire from a heater used to warm water for the cattle, situated in the extreme south end of a connecting shed, and were consumed, together with six young cattle and several hogs. Most of the farming tools were saved. The house was in great danger and was saved only by the most persistent efforts. The contents were removed, it being doubtful whether it could be saved. A large quantity of ice packed for creamery use, (but not covered) between the house and the burning building, was of great assistance in saving the house, the men being able to stand under its shelter at the most critical time, when the fire was nearest, and throw water on the house with small force pumps. No insurance on buildings or contents. The roofs of Rev. Solomon Clark's buildings on the opposite side of the road, repeatedly took fire, but were extinguished.—The saw-mill of Geo. W. Billings, with all its contents, were burned on the night of April 18, 1890. They had been blasting logs for fuel, in the mill yard, during the day, and it is thought that fire might in some way have been communicated to the sawdust in or near the mill. No insurance. The mill has been rebuilt, Mr. Billings being aided in it somewhat by the town's people.—Sept. 18, 1890, the barns of W. E. Shaw were consumed with some sixty or more tons of hay. Insurance on barns, $500; on hay, $500. The cause of the fire is unknown. These barns were on the place formerly occupied by the late William Warner.—The blacksmith shop of J. & E. Spearman took fire on the roof in June, 1878, but was barely saved from destruction by great exertions on the part of the citizens.—July 4, 1888, J. W. Sears' house took fire on the roof. Fortunately it was about dinner time and most of the neighbors were at home, and rallied so quickly that the fire was extinguished before great damage was done. The Insurance company awarded him $60. The town has no apparatus for extinguishing fires. A large public cistern holding many barrels of water, and kept filled by a never-failing stream, was placed near Mack's store, at least 50 years ago, and is still kept up. A similar one was placed near the Town Hall in 1890.

CHAPTER XIII.

PERSONS NOW LIVING HERE OVER 75.—FOREIGNERS.—OLD HOUSES.—GENERAL TYPE. —ORIGINAL DWELLINGS NOW STANDING.—SINGING SCHOOLS.-·"THE OLD VILLAGE CHOIR."—DRAMATIC CLUB.—"SADDLE THE DOGS."—CONTRAST.

Names and ages of persons over 75, living in Plainfield March 14, 1891 :

Mrs. Temperance Atkins,	92	Ira Mason,	76
Isaac T. Barker,	82	Isaac Parker, (about)	80
Sumner Burt,	75	James Spearman, (about)	83
Leonard Campbell,	80	Hiram Stearns,	81
Mrs. L. Campbell,	76	Lyman K. Thayer,	79
Levi Clark,	88	Samuel B. Thayer,	75
Mrs. Levi Clark,	88	Russell Tirrell,	76
Mrs. Susan Cook,	88	Jeremiah Tyrrell,	82
Millson S. Colburn,	83	Thos. K. Wheeler,	78
Mrs. Roxana Dunham,	77	Wm. C. Whiting,	78
Bethuel Gloyd,	81	Mrs. Nancy Williams,	83
Mrs. Martha Hamlen,*	85	William Winslow,	78
Mrs. Margaret Knipping,	85	Emalvin Wing,	83

FOREIGNERS.

Very few foreigners have become permanent residents of this town. James and Edward Spearman, Irish, and by trade blacksmiths, settled here about 1854. Neither were ever naturalized and therefore did not vote. They were industrious, respectable citizens, and amassed quite

---
*Mrs Hamlen died May 17, 1891.

a competence. Edward died in October, 1887. James still lives here, his sister, Margaret Knipping, keeping house for him.—Neil Swanson, a Swede, came here with his family about 1888. His father and mother followed in 1890. Carl and Swan Petterson, relatives of Swanson, also arrived here about the same time as Swanson. They are all industrious, peaceable citizens, most of them fairly well educated. The above named are all the foreigners now living in town.

OLD HOUSES.

The first frame houses built were nearly all of the same style and general plan; one story in height, front door in center, opening into a small entry about 4x8. This opened on each side into a front room about 16x16; each of these into a kitchen and general living room at the back of the house about 20x16. At the gable end of the house, was a door opening into an entry 4x9, at one side of which a flight of narrow and steep stairs ascended to the floor above. At the end of this entry, a door opened into the great kitchen. By the side of this entry door was the entrance to the cellar; just beyond a door opened to a bedroom about 8x9. At the opposite end of the room was a door opening to another bedroom somewhat larger, and by the side of it a "buttery" of ordinary size. A door from the back of the kitchen led to a back room or woodshed, in a separate building. In the center of the house was the capacious chimney, 8 or 10 feet square at the base, by the side of which were cupboards in each of the front rooms, and a big brick oven in the kitchen. A small closet usually opened from the front entry. The windows were high above the floor, and those in the principal rooms contained 24 lights of 6x8 glass; those in the bedrooms and buttery, 15 lights. Two bedrooms with very low ceilings were usually finished off in the chamber. All the nails used were forged by hand and were quite expensive. This description fits nine out of ten of the first frame houses, many of which are still standing. Some have been remodelled by taking out the original chimney and substituting a modern one, changing the interior somewhat. Of those now remaining in nearly their original condition I will name the following : Thos. Mason's, in the southwest part of the town. Original occupant, Ashur Holdridge. Further north on West St., Lemuel Mason's, formerly occupied by Samuel Thayer, Jr. In the east part, on Grant St., the Benj. Gloyd house, unoccupied. On South St., Bethuel Gloyd's, formerly occupied by his father, Joseph Gloyd. On Central St., just south of the village, the house occupied by the family of the late Lewis Shaw and L. A. White, formerly occupied by Josiah Shaw, Jr. This is in the best preservation of any of its class in town. Just south of this is the house built by Josiah first, where his son Freeman lived, but the large chimney has been removed. One fourth of a mile east of this, on Broom St., is that of O. C. Burt, also well preserved. Former occupant Jared Dyer. At the end of Parsons Av. is the house of Stephen Parsons, one of the oldest ; built and occupied by Jacob Nash. South of the meeting-house, on Union St., is the house of James F. Gurney. This has been modernized somewhat by the addition of a piazza, and large windows have been substituted for the old style. The essential features remain, including the chimney. This was formerly occupied by Ichabod Noyes and others. The house of E. A. Atkins, on High St., was built and occupied by John Hamlen. It was thoroughly constructed of the best materials, and the workmanship was better than ordinary. It is now in excellent condition. The Rev. Moses Hallock house, occupied by James Spearman. Mrs. Martha J. Lamb in an article in the Magazine of American History, writes of this house as follows: "A volume could be written with this picturesque old dwelling for a text, which even now looks very comfortable in its antiquity, surrounded by orchards and shade trees, although shorn of the roses and flowery shrubs which formerly beautified its front yard. If its walls could talk, a host of prominent characters who frequented it in the several decades of its history might be introduced to us. After Mr. Hallock's death it was sold, and became for many years the home of Mrs. Mack, a daughter of Dea. Richards, and her family." The house of L. K. Thayer on Pleasant St., built and occupied by Abram Clark, is still in nearly its original condition. The house occupied by Samuel B. Thayer on South Central St., which Elijah Warner, Sr. built, and where he lived and died, and after him his sons Cushing and Wells. The Dea. James Richards house, still standing and in good condition, is occupied by A. B. Cole. The old chimney has been taken out and some minor alterations made in the interior. The house of C. W. Packard on West Hill, original occupant, Josiah Torrey. From this the chimney has been removed. The old Robinson house on Summit St., and N. K. Lincoln's on Pleasant St., are also of this type. The house of S. H. Sears just north of the meeting-house, was built and occupied by Samuel Streeter, and is believed to be the oldest house now standing. It was extensively re-modelled by Cyrus Joy, Esq., some sixty years ago. He added a second story, built four chimnies, and altered the interior so that scarcely any of the original features remain. These houses were all built from 90 to 100 years ago, and as a rule were painted red.

Charles Dudley Warner, in reply to an invitation to be present at the centennial of the Plainfield church in 1886, wrote as follows: "I was very young when I left Plainfield and I have only occasionally visited it of late years, but it has an interest for me that no other place on earth has. The older I grow the more grateful I am that I was born in Massachusetts and in that particular hill-town. I think I owe to its pure air, its noble scenery, the early purity and simplicity of its manners and the influence of an honorable, God-fearing ancestry, the best that is in my life. I was baptized by the splendid old Puritan pastor of that day, Parson Hallock. He was in the best sense the conscience of the town. Scholar, minister, pastor, counselor, who can measure the influence of such a man on his generation! There is the old red house. I should advise everybody to be born in a red house such as that in which I was born, with its rows of fruit trees, its maple orchard, its sunny fields and the stone walls that speak as a fence of wood never can, of security and home."

"From the weather-worn house on the brow of the hill,
We are dwelling afar in our manhood today;
But we see the old gables and hollyhocks still,
As they looked long ago, ere we wandered away;
We can see the tall well-sweep that stands by the door
And the sunshine that gleams on the old yellow floor.

We can hear the low hum of the hard-working bees
At their toil in our father's old orchard once more,
In the broad, trembling tops of the bright blooming trees,
As they busily gather their sweet winter store;
And the murmuring brook,—the delightful old horn,
And the cawing black crows that are pulling the corn.

OLD HOUSES.

We can hear the sharp creak of the farm gate again
And the loud-cackling hens in the gray barn near by
With its broad sagging floor and its scaffolds of grain,
And its rafters, that once seemed to reach to the sky;
We behold the great beams and the bottomless bay
Where we farm boys once joyfully jumped on the hay.

We can see the low hog-pen, just over the way,
And the long, ruined shed by the side of the road,
Where the sleds in the summer were hidden away,
And the wagons and plows in the winter were stowed;
And the cider-mill down in the hollow below,
With a long, creaking sweep, the old horse used to draw,
Where we learned, by the homely old tub, long ago,
What a world of sweet rapture there was in a straw;
From the cider casks there, loosely lying around,
More leaked from the bung-holes than dripped on the ground.

We behold the bleak hillsides still bristling with rocks,
Where the mountain stream murmured with musical sound,
Where we hunted and fished, where we chased the red fox,
With lazy old house dog or loud baying hound;
And the cold, cheerless woods we delighted to tramp
For the shy, whirring partridge, in snow to our knees,
Where, with neck-yoke and pails, in the old sugar-camp
We gathered the sap from the tall maple trees.

And the fields where our plows danced a furious jig,
While we wearily followed the furrow all day,
Where we stumbled and bounded o'er boulders so big
That it took three yoke of oxen to draw them away;
Where we sowed, where we hoed, where we cradled and mowed,
Where we scattered the swaths that were heavy with dew,
Where we tumbled, we pitched, and behind the tall load,
The broken old bull-rake reluctantly drew.

How we grasped the old sheepskin with feelings of scorn
As we straddled the back of the old sorrel mare,
And rode up and down through the green rows of corn
Like a pin on a clothes-line that sways in the air;
We can hear our stern father reproving us still,
As the careless old creature " comes down on a hill."

We are far from the home of our boyhood to-day,
In the battle of life we are struggling alone;
The weather-worn farmhouse has gone to decay,
The chimney has fallen, its swallows have flown,
But Fancy yet brings on her bright golden wings
Her beautiful pictures again from the past,
And Memory fondly and tenderly clings
To pleasures and pastimes, too lovely to last.

We wander again by the river today;
We sit in the school-room o'erflowing with fun,
We whisper, we play, and we scamper away
When our lessons are learned and the spelling is done.

We see the old cellar where apples were kept,
The garret, where all the old rubbish was thrown,
The little back chamber where snugly we slept,
The homely old kitchen, the broad hearth of stone,
Where apples were roasted in many a row,
Where our grandmothers nodded and knit long ago.

Our grandmothers long have reposed in the tomb;
With a strong, healthy race they have peopled the land;
They worked with the spindle, they toiled at the loom,
Nor lazily brought up their babies by hand.

The old flint lock musket, whose awful recoil
Made many a Nimrod in agony cry,
Once hung on the chimney, a part of the spoil
Our gallant old grandfathers captured at "Ti."

Brave men were our grandfathers, sturdy and strong;
The Kings of the forest they plucked from their lands;
They were stern in their virtues, they hated all wrong,
And they fought for the right with their hearts and their hands.

Oh! fresh be their memory, cherished the sod
That long has grown green o'er their sacred remains,
And grateful our hearts to a generous God
For the blood and the spirit that flows in our veins.

Our *Hallocks*, our *Whites*, and our *Warners* are gone
But our mountains remain with their evergreen crown,
The souls of our fathers are yet " marching on,"
The structure they founded shall never go down.

From the weather-worn house on the brow of the hill
We are dwelling afar in our manhood to-day;
But we see the old gables and hollyhocks still,
As they looked when we left them to wander away.
But the dear ones we loved in the sweet long ago
In the old village churchyard sleep under the snow."

EUGENE J. HALL.

SINGING SCHOOLS.

As early as 1794, three choristers were chosen "for the Church and Congregation," viz.: Capt. James Richards, Lieut. Joseph Joy and Ensign Thomas Shaw. In 1798 it was voted to raise $30 for the support of a singing

SINGING SCHOOLS. 119

school. An appropiation of $25 was also made in 1804, to be expended for the same purpose, under the direction of Josiah Shaw, Capt. Joseph Joy and John Hamlen. James Richards led the singing for many years. Later Dea. Freeman Hamlen and Capt. Reuben Hamlen were choristers; afterward, Wm. J. Shattuck, Horatio A. Shaw and others. David Shaw and Orson S. White were the first to introduce the violin into the choir. Dexter White brought in the base-viol about the same time. Orson played the violin in the choir about fifty years in succession, except a few years when he was living in Springfield. Joseph L. Campbell and Seth W. Clark each played the violin with the choir for a few years. Leonard Campbell played the flute and also the double bass-viol for a time. These instruments were some years since superseded by the cabinet organ. This was played by Mrs. L. A. White for a time, then by Mrs. Wm. C. Smith. After she removed from town Mrs. A. R. Tirrell filled the place. Mrs. L. A. White is now the regular organist. An active interest was taken in sustaining a good choir and for many years Plainfield excelled in this respect. Among those who taught singing schools here, were G. W. Lucas, Col. Asa Barr, Wm. F. Sherwin, Marshall Q. L. Dickinson, Mr. Harding and Mrs. Sanderson. Mr. Dickinson has for the third time taught a class here the past winter. As long ago as the old meeting-house was standing, as many as 100 were at one time members of the choir. Wm. C. Whiting and wife, both now living in town, were for 58 and 53 years, respectively, active members. Both retain their voices for singing in a remarkable degree. One Ford, was the first who taught music here, with the possible exception of Dea. Richards.

"THE OLD VILLAGE CHOIR."

"I have fancied, sometimes, the Bethel-bent beam
That trembled to earth in the patriarch's dream,
Was a ladder of song in that wilderness rest,
From the pillow of stone to the blue of the blest,
And the angels descending to dwell with us here,
"Old Hundred" and "Corinth" and "China" and "Mear."

"Let us sing to God's praise," the minister said;
All the psalm-books at once fluttered open at "York,"
Sunned their long dotted wings in the words that he read,
While the leader leaped into the tune just ahead,
And politely picked up the key-note with a fork;
And the vicious old viol went growling along
At the heels of the girls, in the rear of the song.

All the hearts are not dead, not under the sod,
That those breaths can blow open to heaven and God!
Ah, "Silver Street" flows by a bright shining road,—
Oh, not to the hymns that in harmony flowed,—
But the sweet human psalms of the old-fashioned choir,
To the girl that sang alto,—the girl that sang air!

Oh, I need not a wing—bid no genii come
With a wonderful web from Arabian loom,
To bear me again up the river of Time;
When the world was in rhythm, and life was its rhyme,
When the streams of the years flowed so noiseless and narrow
That across it there floated the song of the sparrow.

For a sprig of green caraway carries me there,
To the old village church, and the old village choir,
Where, clear of the floor my feet slowly swung,
And timed the sweet pulse of the praise that they sung,
Till the glory aslant from the afternoon sun
Seemed the rafters of gold in God's temple begun!

You may smile at the nasals of old Deacon Brown
Who followed by scent, till he ran the tune down;
And dear Sister Green, with more goodness than grace,
Rose and fell on the tunes as she stood in her place,
And where "Coronation" exultingly flows,
Tried to reach the high notes on the tips of her toes!

To the land of the leal they have gone with their song,
Where the choir and the chorus together belong;
Oh, be lifted, ye gates! Let me hear them again—
Blessed song, blessed singers! forever, Amen!

Benjamin F. Taylor.

DRAMATIC CLUB.

A dramatic club was organized here about 1870. With the assistance of Stephen Hayward, Jr., a drop curtain and stage scenery and fixtures to the value of $300 were purchased. A number of plays were successfully rendered, among them "Uncle Tom's Cabin," and "Paul Pry," all the characters being local members of the club. It has been practically disbanded for several years. The scenery, still in good condition, remains in the town hall. Frank Jenks, who went West nearly twenty years since, was an excellent actor and an enthusiastic member. When "Uncle Tom's Cabin" was played, he took the part of "Phineas Fletcher," and also that of "Legree." At one of the rehearsals, at the point where the escape of Cassy is discovered, he, taking his cue, came on the stage hurriedly and in an excited manner shouted, "Call out my horse, *Saddle the dogs.*" I think none who were present will forget it, or the bursts of unrestrained laughter that followed, mingled with applause, from the company.

CONTRASTS.

I can hardly close without contrasting the every day living of 100 years ago with that of to-day. The food of our grandfathers and grandmothers was rye and indian bread, johnny cake, pork and beans, and potatoes, with other garden vegetables in their season. Pies and cake were esteemed luxuries and were only had at Thanksgiving time or a wedding. Wheat flour in the earlier days was almost unheard of, but little wheat being raised here. No flour was brought into town for sale until 1812, when a few barrels were brought from New York State. Once or twice a week the capacious brick oven at the side of the chimney was heated by building a fire in it of "oven wood," fine and dry. After the fire had burned down, the coals and ashes were withdrawn, the oven swept with an "oven broom," and the bread, pork and beans and whatever articles were to be baked, placed inside. A "bread peel," which was a broad, flat, long-handled wooden shovel, was used for placing and removing articles from the back of the oven, which was some five feet in diameter. This oven, although it would now be considered very inconvenient, surpassed all the modern stoves and ranges in its baking qualities. The table was set with wooden or pewter plates, the parents and older members of the family only being seated, it being customary at that time for the children to stand during the meal. The houses were heated and cooking, except baking, was done at open fireplaces, which consumed fabulous amounts of wood. They were large enough to take a "back log" 12 or 15 inches in diameter and at least six feet in length. In front of this, on huge andirons, was placed the "fore stick," perhaps one-half as large, with fine wood underneath. The oldest houses were constructed in such a way that a horse could be used to draw the immense back log into the house. It usually lasted two or three days. The fire when once kindled was not allowed to go out from one year's end to the other, the coals at bedtime and at such other times as the fire was not needed, being carefully covered with ashes to keep it. Matches were then unknown, and if by accident or oversight a family lost their fire, a child was dispatched to the nearest neighbors with a skillet or small iron kettle to borrow some live cloals, or if the distance from neighbors was too great, the flint and steel and a little tow were resorted to. Matches when first introduced were only

CONTRASTS.

used in emergencies and cost 25 cents for a small box containing perhaps 50. They were called "Lucifers." Nearly everything in the way of clothing was made from cloth produced at home. Linen and tow cloth from flax raised on the farm, with home-made flannel, supplied the underwear. Men and boys dressed in homespun wool cloth, either blue or butternut color. This cloth after being woven at home, was sent to a cloth-dressing machine, where it was fulled and dressed. The ladies perhaps had a chintz gown purchased at the store for Sunday wear, and the "goodman," if well-to-do, had a broadcloth coat, the material for which had been imported. The boots and shoes for the whole family were made by the shoemaker, each farmer as a rule furnishing his own leather. It was very common for a shoemaker to travel from house to house with his kit of tools, stopping long enough to make and repair what shoes were required for perhaps six months, for each family. It was also common for a tailoress to travel in the same way. Such a thing as buying a pair of shoes at a store was unheard of. Not until as late as 1825 or 1830 were any kept for sale, and then only a few "prunell" shoes for ladies. The loom and large and small spinning wheel were among the most necessary household furnishings. The plows were made of wood, covered by a blacksmith with iron plates. Cast iron plows when first introduced were treated with ridicule, few believing that they could be used in this stony land without being broken at once. Only a few cows were kept, enough to supply butter, milk and cheese for family use, there being little or no outside market for butter. Every farmer kept a flock of sheep, the surplus wool selling readily. Each registered with the town clerk a description of his ear-mark for sheep, which must be different from any previously registered. Much attention was paid to raising, mating, and "breaking" steers; ox teams being much more extensively used than now. They were almost the only team used for all farm purposes.—The usual form of salutation to a superior in social position, or when it was desired to show respect, was "Your sarvant, sir," or "Your sarvant, marm," with a lifting of the hat if by a gentleman, or a courtesy if by a lady. Spirituous liquors were at that time made use of by all, even the minister. They were cheap and unadulterated, and the evil effects resulting from their use were not as marked as at the present day. Not a building could be raised, nor any arduous work undertaken without an abundant supply of rum. I am informed by Mr. Levi Clark, who, although 88 years of age, retains his mental faculties in a remarkable degree, that about the year 1820 twelve hogsheads of rum and other liquors were brought into town and sold in a single year, and probably this did not represent the whole amount drank, to say nothing of unlimited quantities of cider. It is not perhaps worth while to present in detail the style and customs of the present age in contrast with the foregoing. We live in an age when improvement makes rapid strides. What is new and wonderful to-day, becomes like a twice told tale to-morrow. We cease to be surprised at any wonderful invention. Let us be thankful that we live in this age, rather than in the so-called "good old days" of our fathers and grandfathers.

HATFIELD EQUIVALENT.

(The following matter taken from the "History of Hawley," by Wm. G. Atkins, came to hand too late for insertion in the proper place.)

In 1659, in consideration of some services rendered, the General Court granted to Mr. Simon Bradstreet (afterward

Governor) 500 acres of land, and the same amount to Maj. Daniel Denison, with the privilege of locating the same "at any place west of the Connecticut River, provided that it be full six miles from the place intended for Northampton meeting-house, upon a straight line." Gov. Bradstreet had first choice and chose Hatfield north meadows, beginning at the north end of the street and running north and west to the ponds. Maj. Denison took his north of the ponds, extending north on the river one mile, and west from the river 250 rods. Immediately after this Hatfield was settled, and the inhabitants began to murmur about these grants. As they were not then set off from Hadley, that town induced Gov. Bradstreet to remove his claim and accept 1000 acres lying north of Maj. Denison's, and in addition they were to pay the Governor 200 pounds. So after the transfer had been made they had a strip three miles long and 250 rods wide, taking all the meadow land on that side the river for three miles. After Hatfield became a separate town she felt uneasy about this possession of so much of her best farm lands. So she petitioned the "Great and General Court" for some redress for her grievance and the legislature in 1744 gave her the lands lying adjacent to Huntstown, now Ashfield, in all 8064 acres, as an equivalent for the lands originally granted to Bradstreet and Denison. The basis of this division of the Hatfield Equivalent was the valuation of estates for taxation, after the manner of the original division of the town of Hatfield in 1684. There were 83 recipients of this bounty which included all the tax-payers of Hatfied at that time. Their names are given in the records, with the number of acres and rods given to each. These proprietors met at Hatfield May 6, 1765, and passed sundry votes in regard to laying out ways through the tract. These ways were all to be four rods wide and so laid as not to divide any proprietor's lot. Only a few of these ways were ever used, and the vacancies left for that purpose were the occasion of numerous disputes in after years among the owners of the abutting lots. The matter was finally settled by a committee chosen by the town for that purpose, so far as concerned that portion of the tract lying in Plainfield.

GENEALOGICAL HISTORY OF THE EARLY SETTLERS AND THEIR DESCENDANTS, WITH ANECDOTES AND SKETCHES.

EBENEZER BISBEE.

Ebenezer Bisbee, one of the first settlers of the town, was born in 1754, probably in Bridgwater, Mass. He served a short time in the Revolutionary army and settled here as early as 1779, on the farm now occupied by Wm. H. Packard, in the southwest part of the town. He was chosen one of the Selectmen in 1788 and served 15 years. Died Jan. 12, 1837.

Children : Isaac, born April 2, 1779; Barton, April 3, 1781; James, Aug. 11, 1783; John, July 3, 1785; Nabby, Aug. 6, 1788; Jennett, Aug. 16, 1790; Arza, Aug. 11, 1792, died Sept. 3, 1796; Galen, Sept. 1, 1797; Mehitable, May 25, 1800.

1. Isaac mar. Martha Robinson, Nov. 6, 1801.
2. Barton mar. Lovina Bird, Oct. 26, 1803.
3. James mar. Polly Packard, Jan. 28, 1807.
4. John mar. Mary Lyon of Goshen, Feb., 1810. He spent most of his life in Plainfield. Died Jan. 10, 1879 in consequence of injuries received by falling down a flight of stairs. He spent his last years with his daughter, Mrs. L. Campbell, his wife having deceased Feb. 25, 1860, at

the age of 72. Children : Eliza M., born Dec. 16, 1810; Jared, Nov. 25, 1812 ; Lovisa, April 18, 1815; Uzal, April 13, 1818; John Foster, April 5, 1821; Cyrus L., June 14, 1828, died Oct. 17, 1838; James D., May 7, 1829.

Eliza mar. Sylvester Higgins of No. Adams, June, 1834.

Jared mar. Hannah Fowler, April 19, 1837. Children : Almon D., born Jan. 8, 1838; Martha H., Oct. 5, 1844; Eliza, Jan. 14, 1846; James D., May 29, 1847; John F., Feb. 15, 1850; Flora E., Jan. 27, 1852.

Lovisa mar. Leonard Campbell, April 15, 1835.

Uzal mar. Olivia Longley of Hawley. Children : Harriet, Alice, Julia and Carrie.

Nabby, daughter of Ebenezer, mar. Rufus P. Bates, Nov. 29, 1804.

Jennett, daughter of Ebenezer, mar. Stephen Hayward, Sept. 11, 1812, died Feb. 2, 1838.

Galen, son of Ebenezer, mar. Penelope Patch, Jan. 1, 1824. Children, born in Plainfield, Lucinda, Nov. 27, 1824.

Mehitable, daughter of Ebenezer, mar. Joel Lyon, March 8, 1821.

JOSEPH BEALS.

Joseph Beals was born in Bridgwater, Mass., in 1752. He came here with his family in 1779, when this town was still a part of Cummington. In 1789, a year of great scarcity, he suffered the loss of his house and nearly all his provisions by fire. His religious experience, dating from this calamity, was the subject of the tract, "The Mountain Miller," by Wm. A. Hallock. It has been printed in the French and German, as well as the English language, and its circulation has reached several hundred thousand copies. The second house which he built is the

JOSEPH BEALS.

same now occupied by Nelson W. Cook, though it has been considerably altered. His grist-mill was a few rods above the present mill of J. A. Nash. Served as selectman in 1795. Was chosen deacon of the Plainfield church in 1803. Died July 20, 1813, aged 61. His children were Samuel, born in Bridgwater, Sept. 26, 1775 ; Joseph, Jr., also born in Bridgwater, July 3, 1778 ; Robert, born Dec. 7, 1780; Lydia L., May 19, 1787, died Dec. 4, 1804; Polly, April 13, 1789; Lovisa, Jan. 4, 1792.

1. Samuel mar. Sally Chamberlain, July 31, 1798. Their children were Dennis, born May 14, 1799; Otis, Dec. 16, 1801; Lydia L., Feb. 10, 1806, mar. Lemuel Allis (second wife) May 18, 1825.—Samuel died June 30, 1851.—Dennis mar. Almira Hadlock in 1821. Their children were Samuel, 2d, born Aug. 8, 1824; Dennis A., Oct. 13, 1827 ; Laura A., March 30, 1831; John C., Jan. 1, 1834 ; Flora E., Nov. 4, 1844, and two who died in infancy.—Samuel, 2d, mar. Miss Bushnell of Cheshire and removed to Michigan, where he died.—Dennis A. mar. Ruth T. Hunt of Hawley, March, 1847. Lives in North Adams.—Laura mar. Lewis Longley, May, 1855; died Jan., 1891.—John C. mar. Lorinda H. Fuller of Hawley, Oct. 1855.—Flora E. mar. Harvey L. Hadlock, June 11, 1868; died Nov. 19, 1868. Almira, wife of Dennis, was for many years insane, but was not so violent as to make it necessary to confine her. Dennis died March 29, 1879.—Otis mar. Roxana Lazell, March 20, 1826. They settled in Hawley. Otis died in Plainfield, June 10, 1882. Children : Edmund, born Dec. 2, 1827, died in Plainfield, Oct. 13, 1862 ; Roxana, Nov. 21, 1830, mar. James Murray, 1857, live in Iowa; H. Harrison, Nov. 5, 1838; H. Wesley, July 20, 1836, mar. Harriet Landon, June, 1859—one son, Fred W., born Oct. 23, 1861,

He mar. Cora H. Hinckley, April 11, 1886—one son, Darwin L., born Dec. 23, 1888.

2. Joseph Beals, Jr. mar. Betsey Reed, May 13, 1802; died Aug. 7, 1847. Children: Harriet, born April 9, 1803; Loren Dec. 6, 1805; Dexter, Oct. 28, 1807; Annis, Jan. 23, 1811, died May 6, 1841; Betsey, Feb. 17, 1814, died June 23, 1839; Lydia P., Feb. 5, 1818; Joseph 3d, Aug. 6, 1821.—Harriet mar. Lorin White, March 31, 1823.—Loren mar. Sarah Davison, Nov. 29, 1832.—Dexter mar. Julia Packard of Goshen.— Joseph 3d married and settled in Greenfield, Mass., as a dentist.

3. Robert mar. Nabby Vining, Jan. 10, 1805. Was chosen one of the Selectmen in 1819 and served four years. Was chosen Town Clerk in 1821, and served seven years. Died July 2, 1844. Children : Fordyce, born Oct. 21, 1806; Vesta, Sept. 29, 1808; Eli V., Jan 25, 1810; Mary, April 12, 1812; Abigail, June 24, 1816; Robert P., Aug. 24, 1819; Alden Porter, May 30, 1825.—Fordyce mar. Mary H. Green, died in New Haven, Ct. in 1870.—Vesta mar. Samuel Snell of Cummington, Dec. 14, 1831. He deceased, and she mar. Philo Packard of Cummington (second wife).—Eli V. died in Pittsfield in 1854.—Mary mar. Albert Dyer, Dec. 3, 1835. —Abigail mar. Granville B. Hall of Ashfield, April 11, 1843.—Robert P. mar. for second wife Margaret Burt, died in Springfield, Oct. 7, 1885.—Alden P. mar. for second wife Augusta Waite of Hatfield, died at Stamford, Ct., April 12, 1889.

4. Polly, daughter of Joseph 1st, mar. Ebenezer Lovell, March 2, 1809, died July 30, 1810.

5. Lovisa, mar. Wm. Reed of Albany, N. Y., Jan. 11, 1814.

JOHN CAMPBELL.

John Campbell was born Nov. 2, 1752. Served in the war of the Revolution, and witnessed Burgoyne's surrender to Gates in 1777. Mar. Lydia Kent, June 25, 1783, and settled here as early as 1784. They lived in a small house on the exact site of the old Campbell house, torn down in 1890. His wife Lydia died Sept. 6, 1806, aged 51. He mar. for a second wife, Betsey Hunt of Hawley, Jan. 18, 1809. She died Sept. 7, 1818, aged 38. For a third wife he mar. Mrs. Asenath Claghorn of Hawley, Nov. 1819. Her daughter by her first husband, Mrs. Temperance Atkins, is still living in town. He died April 25, 1833. Children of John and his wife Lydia were Ebenezer, born July 13, 1784; Levi, March 5, 1786; Edmund, Feb. 19, 1788; Sally, Dec. 8, 1789; Amasa, May 30, 1791; Betsey, July 15, 1797.

1. Ebenezer is not further mentioned in the records. He married and had at least one son, Ebenezer, Jr.

2. Levi mar. Clarissa Joy, daughter of Joseph, June 14, 1810, died Nov. 6, 1874. Children : Leonard, born April 15, 1811,; Levi N., Nov. 13, 1812. Clarissa M., Sept. 16, 1821; Joseph Lyman, Dec. 19, 1824; also a daughter who died in 1818, aged 3, and another in 1828, aged 11.—Leonard mar. Lovisa Bisbee, April 15, 1835. Held the office of Deputy Sheriff for 28 years, and Postmaster over 30 years. Has served as moderator of town meetings more times than any other citizen. Had one son, Fred E., born May 17, 1836. He mar. Amanda L. Pratt, Oct. 30, 1860. They had one child, Kate L., born Sept. 16, 1862; mar. Merritt O. Wallace. Reside in Florence, Mass. Fred E. died in Florence, Mass., Oct. 29, 1886. The following resolutions

were passed by "Florence Lodge, No. 1207, Knights of Honor," on his decease :

"*Whereas*, it has pleased the Supreme Dictator of the Universe, to again invade our circle, and call from the fraternity before to that beyond, Brother Frederick E. Campbell, and

Whereas, in his death our lodge has sustained the loss of a valued and efficient member, the community an honest, upright citizen, his family a kind, loving and faithful husband and father, therefore,

Resolved, that while we bow in humble submission to the Divine Will, we desire to express the deep sense of personal loss we feel, and extend to the afflicted family our earnest and heartfelt sympathy in their great bereavement and sorrow, and say that while we shall see his face no more, his life and example will ever remain to stimulate and bind us more closely together in the ties of our common brotherhood.

Resolved, that our lodge be draped in mourning for thirty days, and that a copy of these resolutions be placed on our records, and a copy be sent to the family of the deceased."

Levi N. mar. Ruth W. Hall of Hawley, May, 1841. Was chosen one of the Selectmen in 1849, and held the office twenty-two years; longer that any other person in the history of the town. He was for the greater part of the time, Chairman of the board. Was chosen a member of the School Committee in 1841, and held the office nineteen years. Represented the town in the legislature in 1854, and the district in 1864. Has for the last ten years resided in Florence, Mass. Children of Levi N. and Ruth were George L., born July 28, 1846; Ruth Florence, Dec. 25, 1850. Ruth, wife of Levi N., deceased Feb. 3, 1851. For a second wife, mar. Rachel Whitmarsh, Nov. 24, 1852. Children. Herbert S., born Nov. 3, 1857; Louis L., Aug. 30, 1859; Addie C., Feb. 29, 1864.

George L. mar. Laura E. Warner, daughter of William, Nov. 27, 1867. Reside in Northampton. Florence cares

for her father, his wife having deceased in January, 1887. Herbert S. mar. Minnie B. Howes, June 10, 1879. Reside in Northampton. Children: Harry N., born June 8, 1880; Cherie M., Sept. 4, 1889.

Louis L. mar. Margie W. Stockwell of Northampton. She deceased in a year or two after their marriage, and in 1890 he mar. Alice S. Spear, also of Northampton. In February, 1877, he became clerk in the Northampton Post Office, under Postmaster Joy. He remained as clerk and Asst. P. M. for about five years, when he was appointed to a position in the railway mail service, and April 1, 1882, went on duty on the route from Palmer, Mass. to Brattleboro', Vt. In Jan., 1883, he was transferred to the line between Boston and New York, via Springfield. Was gradually promoted to higher grades and in May, 1889, was appointed "clerk in charge" of a crew of twelve clerks. This line is considered one of the heaviest in the country, and three postal cars are required on the night trains. He resigned this position in August, 1890, to accept the appointment of Postmaster of Northampton, which office he now holds. During his service as railway postal clerk, he was called upon for twenty-four examinations, each consisting of from 500 to 1000 questions. In fifteen of these he passed 100 per cent., and in the other nine he stood above 99 per cent. As postmaster, he is most thorough and efficient, and has made several important improvements in the service.

Addie C. mar. Chas. Huxley of Florence, in 1888, in which place they now reside.

Clarissa M., daughter of Levi, mar. Thos. D. Clark of Hawley, June 29, 1842.

Joseph L. mar. Adeline C. Eldridge of Hawley, May,

1851. They had one or two children who died in infancy. She deceased, and he married for a second wife, Augusta Eldridge, a sister of the first. They have one daughter, Mary. Reside in Florence, Mass. He was for several years, while in Easthampton, a Deputy Sheriff under Maj. Longley.

3. Edmund, son of John, mar. Nancy Shaw, daughter of Josiah 1st, May 23, 1817. Had one son, Josiah Dwight, born Oct. 30, 1818, and two who died in infancy. He mar. Lucy Adams of Chicopee. Had one daughter, Lizzie S., born Dec. 23, 1844, died Oct. 24, 1861. J. Dwight died Feb. 17, 1849.

4. Sally, daughter of John, mar. William Joy, March, 1810.

5. Amasa mar. Sally Bester, Oct. 14, 1813. Children: Emily B., born Sept. 26, 1815; John T., Feb. 12, 1818; Betsey P., June 1820; Sally M., May 23, 1822.

6. Betsey, daughter of John, mar. Watson Pool of South Hadley, Dec. 5, 1822.

ABRAM CLARK.

Abram Clark was born in Attleboro', Mass., in 1751. Settled in Plainfield not far from 1783, on the farm where L. K. Thayer now lives. His wife was Silence Gloyd, from Abington. He died Nov. 24, 1834. Children : Susanna, born Oct. 19, 1782; Polly, Aug. 5, 1784; Betsey, April 15, 1786; James, Nov. 29, 1787; Lydia, Sept. 4, 1789, died June 7, 1890; Elijah, May 4, 1791; Samuel, Nov. 28, 1792; Abram, Jr., Feb. 22, 1796; Silence, July 2, 1801, died Jan. 13, 1808.

1. Susanna mar. Asa Thayer, Dec. 2, 1804, died March 5, 1870.

2. Polly mar. John Shaw, Jr., Oct. 24, 1802, died April 20, 1808.

3. Betsey mar. Reuben Kingman of Goshen, March 18, 1808.

4. James mar. Zeruah Bigelow of Cummington, March, 1808. Children: Mary Ann, born July 17, 1810, and probably others. He removed from town soon after his marriage and became a minister of the Baptist denomination. His wife deceased and he returned to Plainfield when over 70 years old. At the age of 74 he married Hannah Gurney, (widow of Joseph Gurney and previously of Beza Reed, maiden name Stockwell.) He preached for the Baptist Society for a short time, being their last regular minister, and died July 5, 1868.

5. Elijah mar. Waity Jenks of Cheshire. She died Jan. 17, 1850, and he married for a second wife, Lucretia Lyman of Hadley, July, 1851. He represented the town in the legislature in 1835 and 1836, and was for many years a Justice of the Peace. Died in West Cummington about 1884. Children of Elijah and Waity were John, born Dec. 26, 1813; Minerva, Feb. 4, 1816; Samantha, Oct. 7, 1818; Lewis, Dec. 13, 1822; Elijah Alden, May 12, 1827; James Dwight, July 6, 1830. John mar. Hannah Jones, Dec. 1834, and removed from town.

Samantha mar. Alden W. Mason, Nov. 30, 1837.

Elijah A. mar. Loraine F. Warner, Oct. 30, 1849. Children: Willis A., born Nov., 1850; George W., Aug. 1, 1854.—Loraine F., wife of Elijah A., died Oct. 18, 1854. He married for a second wife, Hannah L. Lyman, Dec. 3, 1856. Their children were Chas. L., born Oct. 2, 1857; Alice L., Oct. 25, 1861.

James Dwight mar. Flora Stevens, Sept. 26, 1851, died

Feb. 1, 1856. They had one child, Flora Ellen, born May 28, 1853.

6. Samuel mar. Lucy Sheldon. Children: Lorinda, born Nov. 17, 1816; Parthena R., Nov. 16, 1819; Polly, Dec. 11, 1821; Samuel Sheldon, Dec. 22, 1823; Eliza Ann, Sept. 19, 1826.

JACOB CLARK.

Jacob Clark was born in Abington, Mass., in 1755. Served in the Revolutionary war and came to Plainfield in 1783. He mar. Susanna Jones, sister of Jacob. They lived on the farm since occupied by his son Chester, where H. H. Fenton now lives. Died July 16, 1832. Children: Hannah, born March 1, 1783; Sarah, Nov. 27, 1784 ; Rebekah, Jan. 17, 1787; Mary, July 9, 1789; David, March 13, 1792, died March 13, 1796; Jacob, Jr., Sept. 22, 1794; Lucy, Sept. 22, 1797; Nancy, Oct. 4, 1799; Levi, Dec. 30, 1802; Chester, May 4, 1805; Alanson, May 14, 1807.

1. Hannah died Nov. 27, 1830.
2. Sarah died March 7, 1813.
3. Rebekah mar. Daniel Coe of Durham, N. Y., Feb. 17, 1822.
4. Mary mar. Rev. James Jewell of Durham, N. Y., July 1, 1816.
5. Jacob, Jr., remained in town and was engaged in woolen manufacturing and trade. He never married. Was chosen Town Clerk in 1841, and served three years. Died Feb. 16, 1848.
6. Lucy died May 12, 1828.
7. Nancy died July 7, 1803.
8. Levi mar. Electa Joy, daughter of Joseph, Oct. 2, 1828. Both are still living in town. He kept store for

JACOB CLARK. 137

some years in company with his brother Jacob, until his death, when he conducted the business alone for seven or eight years. He was Postmaster some four years, and had charge of the office about eight years. Was chosen Town Clerk in 1848, and held the office five years. Children: Mary J., born May 9, 1830, mar. Wm. H. Dyer, May 18, 1854; Charles C., born Dec. 12, 1836. He has not married yet.

9. Chester mar. Minerva Jones, daughter of Jacob, Dec. 1, 1831, and remained on the old homestead, died March 18, 1885. Children: Seth W., born Sept. 22, 1833; Elizabeth S., Sept. 19, 1842. Seth W. mar. Nancy W. Jones, Sept. 3, 1855. They lived for some years after their marriage in Brooklyn, N. Y., but returned to Plainfield about 1862, where they have since resided. He was chosen one of the Selectmen in 1873, and has served six years in all, being Chairman for several years. Has served 13 years as one of the School Committee, being elected to that office in 1863. He is at present, president of the Cummington Creamery Association, an office which he has held since the formation of company. Was chosen deacon of the Cong. Church, March 3, 1877. Children: Nellie M., born in 1857; Fred D., 1860, both born in Brooklyn, N. Y.; Henry D., born Oct. 26, 1865; Alice C., May 8, 1868; Marian N., June 2, 1870 ; Frank S., June 27, 1873, died Jan. 28, 1875.

Nellie M. mar. Arthur R. Tirrell, Nov. 27, 1879.

Fred D. mar. C. Helen Gurney of Cummington, June 23, 1885. Children: Etha Helen, born June 23, 1886.

10. Alanson never married. Was by trade a tailor, and lived in the family of his brother Chester. Died Oct. 10, 1883.

ANDREW COOK.

Andrew Cook was born in 1737. Was one of the very earliest settlers, having come here previous to 1774. He lived on the place since occupied by Horace Daniels, east of Dea. S. W. Clark's; died March 6, 1814. Children: Hannah, born Oct. 6, 1774; John, Oct. 18, 1776. These two were, so far as known, the first of each sex born in the present town limits. They both died in infancy or early childhood. His other children were John 2d, born Oct. 27, 1778; Joseph, Feb. 1, 1781; Hannah 2d, Nov. 13, 1783. He also had daughters, Sarah, Lois and Amy, whose names do not appear on the town records.

1. John mar. Susanna Gurney, Sept. 15, 1796. He was by trade a carpenter and builder and many of the oldest houses now standing were built by him, as well as others of later construction. Children: Thomas, born May 23, 1801; Edson, May 27, 1803; James, March 29, 1805; Roswell, July 9, 1811; Benjamin F., March 25, 1815; John Jackson, Sept. 24, 1817, besides three daughters who died in childhood.—Thomas mar. Rachel Gurney of Ashfield, Jan. 1824, and settled in Cummington. Died April 16, 1856. Children: Elmira and Elvira, twins, mar. John Snow and Alonzo Eldridge; Henry W., mar. Selina Shaw; Sarah D.; Rachel, mar. Ansel B. Cole, Feb., 1856; Lovina and Martin L. Martin was a member of the 52d Mass. Reg't in the late war, and died Sept. 8, 1863, aged 27.—Edson mar. Esther Abel of Goshen, Feb., 1824. Died suddenly while crossing the field between Jared Dyer's house and the village, Feb. 5, 1858. He had been dead some hours when discovered. Children: Maria E., born Feb. 15, 1825; James Edward, Sept. 9, 1826; Edson, Jr., April 8, 1831; Alfred E., May 16, 1839; Susan E., May 27, 1844.

James Cook mar. Susan Joy, daughter of Isaac, Jr., Jan. 24, 1833. They lived on the homestead formerly occupied by Joseph Beals, the " Mountain Miller." Died Oct. 21, 1881. Children: Harriet, born Oct. 27, 1833; Andrew S., July 31, 1837; Nelson W., March 29, 1840; Franklin, June 30, 1843.—Harriet mar. C. Wells Smith of Worthington, June 18, 1851.—Andrew S. mar. Addie M. Livermore of Peru, Dec. 1862. They reside in Springfield, Mass.—Nelson W. mar. Mary E. Davison, Nov. 2, 1864. They live on the old homestead, which he has greatly improved; his mother, aged 88, living with them. Was a member of the 37th Mass. Reg't in the late war.—Franklin entered the army and died in the service at Beaufort, N. C., June 20, 1863. James and his son Nelson W. were both carpenters. It was the family trade.

Roswell mar. Elsie Thayer, Aug. 19, 1830, died March 27, 1881. Children: Laura A., born Feb. 10, 1831; John F., June 12, 1835; Royal, Dec. 25, 1837; and Flora.

Benj. F. mar. Abigail Bates, Oct. 11, 1836, died Aug. 31, 1842. Children: Martha and Jared Allen.

John Jackson mar. Irene Rice of Hawley. Children: Mary, Joseph, William and Adrian.—The wife of John, son of Andrew, died Sept. 18, 1836. For a second wife he married Hannah Packard, daughter of Caleb Packard of Ashfield, May 30, 1838. He died July 9, 1849.

2. Joseph mar. Sally Joy, Sept. 19, 1799. Children: Levi, Jason, Laura, Clarissa, Electa and Bennett.

3. Hannah, daughter of Andrew, mar. Jacob Gardner, Jr., Feb. 20, 1806.

JESSE DYER.

We quote the following from Hobart's History of Abington :—" The name Dyer was doubtless originally given to designate some individual by his occupation. It occurs in English records as early as 1436, and I know not how much earlier. The Dyers were of English origin; the name occurs in the Yorkshire pedigrees. George Dyer of Dorchester came over in the "Mary and John," May, 1630. William Dyer petitioned to be made a freeman, in Weymouth, in 1635 or 1636. He removed to Rhode Island in 1638. From him the Dyers of that state are descended. The Dyers of Connecticut sprung from John and Thomas, who settled in Windham county. They were sons of Thomas Dyer of Weymouth, who is supposed to have settled there about 1632. The coat-of-arms of the Dyer family was a plain shield, surmounted by a wolf's head, as appears from a tombstone in the burying ground on Copp's Hill, Boston. I find the name very often occurs among the tradesmen and mechanics of England, and is abundant in the Post Office Directory of London. There are many of the name in Maine, descendants of Asa (brother of Jesse) and also on the Cape, descended from the same original stock."

Although Jesse Dyer lived just over the line in Ashfield, quite a portion of his farm was in Plainfield, he attended church there, his sons all settled there, and he himself in his last years removed there. He was born in Abington, Mass., in 1769. His father and grandfather were named Christopher. He came to Ashfield soon after 1790, and settled on the farm where Benjamin M. Dyer now lives. This, like the rest of the town, was heavily covered with woods. He cleared a few acres, built a small house and a barn, and married Sally Pool, daughter of Dea. Samuel Pool, Oct. 4, 1795. Children: Jared, born Nov. 1, 1796; Oakes, Feb. 22, 1799; Bela, May 24, 1802; Albert, June 25,

1807; Sarah, about 1810; Samuel, July 23, 1813; Newell, Jan. 23, 1818, and one who died in infancy in 1805.

1. Jared mar. Olive Pool, daughter of Benjamin, Oct. 14, 1824. Lived where O. C. Burt now lives; died Feb. 25, 1874. Children: Wm. H., born Sept. 13, 1825; Betsey Ann, June 21, 1827, died Aug. 22, 1828; Edwin J., June 3, 1829; Emily G., Oct. 14, 1834; Alfred T., July 19, 1839. Wm. H. mar. Mary J. Clark, May 18, 1854.—Edwin J. mar. Marion Cole, May 4, 1853; died Jan. 2, 1882.—Emily G. mar. J. Morton Barber, Oct. 11, 1857. Have for many years lived in Pittsfield, Mass., Mr. Barber having been employed for more than 25 years by Rice, Robbins & Co. —Alfred T. mar. Emily M. Stowell of Hinsdale, Mass., July 3, 1864. She deceased Aug. 21, 1866, and he married for a second wife Emily C. Wentworth of Hinsdale, March 20, 1867. Has been for a number of years overseer of the extensive farm of W. H. Milton at Pittsfield, Mass.

2. Oakes mar. Electa Stoddard Nov., 1824. They lived on the place originally occupied by Thomas Shaw, just below the Jared Dyer place. About 1855 he bought the Dr. Porter house, which stood on the corner south of the "Brick store," and removed it to his place. As soon as it was ready to occupy, the brick house in which he at first lived, was torn down. No buildings now remain on the place except a barn. Children: Electa S., born Jan. 26, 1826; Spencer O., Oct. 4, 1827; Lewis S., Jan. 4, 1829; Angeline M., Oct. 4, 1831; Julia M., Feb. 19, 1842.—Electa mar. Francis K. Cottrell, Oct. 20, 1852, died Oct. 11, 1862. —Spencer O. mar. Elizabeth A. Ely of Westfield, Mass., Aug., 1855. Studied for the ministry and after preaching for Congregational churches for a few years, he joined the Methodist denomination, under which he preached until

quite recently. He is now, or has quite recently been teaching in the High schools near Boston.—Lewis S. mar. Mary L. Porter of Hatfield, March, 1853. Has resided in Hatfield, Mass., since his marriage.—Angeline mar. Geo. W. Cottrell of Worthington, May, 1854. Went to live in Middlefield.—Julia died in Middlefield, Dec. 5, 1883. She was unmarried. Electa, first wife of Oakes, died March 4, 1842, aged 41. For a second wife he married Mrs. Nabby V. Taylor of Hawley, widow of Zebulon Taylor, March, 1844. She died Nov. 27, 1846, aged 48. For a third wife he married Mary Ford of Windsor, Aug., 1850. She died April 8, 1858, aged 56. He died in Middlefield, Jan. 28, 1877.

3. Bela mar. Deborah White, daughter of Samuel, in 1824. They settled on the farm where John F. Cook lives. Children: Mary Ann, born Feb. 28, 1825; Marantha, May 28, 1827. His wife died Nov. 16, 1828. For a second wife he married Ruth Ranney of Ashfield, Dec. 22, 1830. Children: Charles B., born 1832, died March 8, 1834, being choked by a piece of apple lodged in his windpipe; Newell 2d, born Feb. 27, 1835; Newcomb, Jan. 15, 1837. Both served in the Union army in the late war, Newell in the 31st Mass., Newcomb in the 46th.—Mary Ann mar. Jonathan Brackett, Feb. 29, 1850. They lived in Searsburg, Vt. for some years, where Mr. Brackett conducted a tannery. They removed to Schroon Lake, N. Y., where he died Feb. 2, 1884. She married Wm. Henry Packard of this town Oct. 26, 1887, and now resides here.

Marantha mar. Sylvester S. Hall, Nov. 18, 1847. They lived in Hawley and Conway and finally in Williamsburg, where he died, July 5, 1868. She married Rev. Wakefield Gale of Easthampton, Aug. 31, 1879. He deceased Oct. 2, 1881. She now resides with her son in Iowa.

Newell 2d, mar. Marion Granger Jan. 1, 1863. She died Oct. 8, the same year. Had one daughter, Nettie A., born Sept. 30, 1863; deceased. For a second wife he married Ellen Joy of Peru, Oct., 1866. She died Nov. 14, 1881. Children: Frank B., born Feb. 17, 1868; Adelbert N., April 13, 1877. For a third wife he married Rose Thayer of Hawley, in which town they now reside. Frank B., son of Newell 2d, while laboring under a fit of temporary insanity, shot himself through the head with a revolver, near Amity, Mo., in 1889, at which place he had just arrived on a visit to relatives. He died instantly.

Newcomb mar. Julia A. Thayer, Feb. 4, 1864. She died Aug. 1, 1867. Children: Fordyce N., born April 28, 1865; Alden M., July 30, 1867. He married for a second wife, Harriet E. Thayer, Aug. 30, 1868. They removed to DeKalb Co. (near Amity) Missouri, where they have reared a large family and still reside.

Ruth, second wife of Bela, died Sept. 6, 1863, aged 57. He for a third wife married Mary Nash of Madison, Ohio, widow of Vinson Nash, and sister of his first wife, June 2, 1865. In the spring of 1869 he removed to North Madison, O., where he died, Aug. 19, 1878. While most of the Dyer brothers were what might be called " original characters," Bela was perhaps the most widely known, and will be more generally remembered than any other. He was a very fluent talker, and a great story teller. Although a man of truth in all ordinary matters, he had a well known habit of exaggerating a story, which was highly amusing to his listeners. Rev. Moses Hallock once mildly remonstrated with him. " I know it," said Uncle Bela, with tears in his eyes, touched by the kind reproof, " I know it, and I've shed *hogsheads* of tears over it." His stories must have been heard from his lips in order to be fully appreciated. The roll of his eye, the clip of one hand over the other, his solemn manner at the close, as though he was testifying in court under oath, and his gestures, can not be re-produced. A few of his stories I will endeavor to write out.

A GREAT SLAUGHTER.

The house where he lived soon after his first marriage was infested with rats. A room in the second story was used for storing corn. The rats had effected an entrance at one corner, and were making sad havoc with it, their excursions being of course mainly at night. Uncle Bela determined to have their blood; so he arranged a swinging cover to the rat hole with strings connected which he carried through small holes in the ceiling over the head of his bed in the room underneath, so that he could grasp them and open or close the hole as he wished. At night when he retired he pulled a string and left the hole open. About midnight he was awakened by the noise of a small army of rats in the room overhead. He closed the hole by the string, rose, partially dressed, and taking a convenient club and a candle ascended to the chamber, where the rats were holding carnival, and closing the door he valiantly attacked his foes, nor stayed his hand till every rat had bit the dust. He then opened the hole and returned to bed, where, wearied with his efforts, he soon fell asleep. About 2 A. M. he was again awakened by the noise of another detachment of rats rolling the ears of corn overhead. He quickly closed the aperture, rose, again ascended the stairs, and the first scene was repeated. As he closed the door and again descended to bed, he was reminded of Samson's slaughter of the Philistines. "In the morning," said he, "I thought I'd go and pick up the dead rats, so I took a bushel basket and went up and as I was a pickin' on 'em up I thought I'd *count* 'em. So I done so, an' ther was *four hundred and fifty.*" I have learned from Mr. Levi Clark who lived neighbor to him at the time, that the main points in the story are true, but he had increased the original number at least ten-fold.

A SLIPPERY TIME.

He was often called to serve on a jury and at one time in the winter when he was attending court there came a rain storm which froze as it fell, covering everything with glare ice. Said he, "I came out o' the court house and down the steps a leetle ahead o' the other jurymen. I had taken a few steps on the sidewalk when my heels went Zip! and I went down. I rolled my eye 'round behind me to see if anybody had seen me fall, and behold! *every one* of the other eleven jurymen sat flat on the sidewalk in a row, one behind 'tother."

HE HAD STRONG LUNGS.

"Talkin' about light snows," said Uncle Bela, taking a huge chew of fine cut, "one night in the winter about twenty years ago I went to bed as usual. The stars shone bright and a clearer night I never saw. When I got up in the morning it was still clear as a bell, but on going to the door I found there had *four feet* of snow fallen in the night. I see 'twas pretty light, so I put my head down and blew one puff. It blew a hole *clean to the ground.* The whole on't, if 'twas well squeezed down, wouldn't made *a half an inch.*"

DURABLE TIMBER.

A neighbor was about new-silling his barn. Said Uncle Bela, "Why don't you get a red beech? It will last *five hundred years. I've tried it twice.*"

A CORRECT TIMEPIECE.

He had an old-fashioned tall clock which he set great store by. Said he, "That clock will run nine hundred years and not vary *the thickness of a case knife.*"

TRULY DEPLORABLE.

In speaking of the deplorable condition of the heathen in a certain country, he said, "They eat *old shoes;* don't know whether they've got a maker *above or below.*"

4. Albert mar. Mary Beals, daughter of Dea. Robert and grand-daughter of the "Mountain Miller," Dec. 3, 1835. They settled where Sumner Burt now lives in the east part of the town. About the time of Dea. Robert Beals' death they removed to his house and cared for his widow until her death and made their permanent residence there. He was chosen one of the School Committee in 1840 and served thirteen years. Also chosen Selectman the same year, and served four years. Was appointed Justice of the Peace as early as 1860, and held the office until his death, which occurred July 16, 1883. His widow still retains the old homestead which was occupied by her father, spending the summer there and the remainder of the year with her daughter in Conway. Their children were Flora A., born Feb. 26, 1838, died Sept. 7, 1855; Mary F. and Fordyce A., twins, born Nov. 8, 1840. Mary was a successful teacher in this and other towns. Married W. D.

Sanderson of Conway, Dec. 9, 1875. He died a few years since. She and her children still reside in Conway. Fordyce entered Williams college in 1861, but left before graduating to enter the army, where (as related elsewhere) he died Oct. 26, 1864.

5. Sarah mar. Ebenezer Crosby of Hawley, June 13, 1833. They removed to Wisconsin where she died in 1848, leaving several children.

6. Samuel mar. Mrs. Martha Hamlen Cole of Worthington, June, 1837. Lived where C. N. Holden now lives. Served as Selectman in 1855, and School Committee in 1848; died April 9, 1883. Children: Alden H., born June 19, 1839; Augusta M., May 19, 1841; Effie G., July 15, 1850.—Alden mar. Nancy L. Barber, Dec. 29, 1861. He entered the army in 1862 and died in the service at Newbern, N. C., Jan. 19, 1863.—Effie mar. Chas. N. Holden of Hawley, May 4, 1872. They reside on the old homestead of Samuel Dyer, her sister Augusta living with them.

7. Newell, youngest son of Jesse, mar. Mary Ann Whitmarsh, May 24, 1842. Remained with his parents caring for them until their death; his mother dying March 24, 1852, aged 73, and his father July 13, 1854, aged 85. Lived on the old place until 1847, when he purchased the Dea. James Richards farm, and removed thither, where he remained eight years. In 1856 he removed to the village. His wife died May 2, 1866. For a second wife he married Mrs. Lydia L. Sears, widow of Wm. H. Sears of Ashfield, Oct. 17, 1866. He deceased Feb. 23, 1872. Had one son, Charles N., born Jan. 7, 1850. Was chosen Town Clerk and Treasurer in 1876, which offices he has held until the present time. Was chosen a member of the School Committee in 1872, served ten years and is at pres-

ent a member of the board. Appointed a Justice of the Peace in 1884, and Postmaster in 1889. Married M. Antoinette Ford of Peru, Oct. 6, 1872. Children: Albert F., born Aug. 2, 1873; L. Genevieve, June 7, 1880; Charles Frederick, Aug. 16, 1882.

JOSEPH GLOYD.

Joseph Gloyd was born in Abington, Mass., in 1763. Served a short time in the Revolutionary army, and settled here about 1790. Married Abigail Garnett of this town, Dec. 6, 1792, and settled on the place where his son Bethuel now lives. Died July 15, 1842. His brothers, Benjamin and Ephraim, settled here about the same time. All were physically, large heavy men. Benjamin, Sr. at his death weighed about 300 lbs. It is related that it was found necessary to widen the doorway by removing the casing from one side, in order to take the coffin from the house decently at the time of his funeral. Children of Joseph were Levi, born Aug. 24, 1793; Betsey, Nov. 27, 1797; Lovisa, April 29, 1800; Albina, May 3, 1803; Joseph, Jr., May 29, 1806; Bethuel, Sept. 13, 1809.

1. Levi mar. Wealthy Bates of Hawley, June, 1816, died Aug. 29, 1819. Had one son, Charles Lewis, born Dec. 26, 1819.

2. Betsey mar. Ahaz Robbins of Cummington, June 26, 1817.

3. Lovisa mar. James Snow of Cummington, May, 1821.

4. Albina mar. Norman White, June 20, 1821.

5. Joseph Jr., mar. Annis Thayer, Sept. 17, 1829, died Dec. 19, 1880. Children: Albina, born April 7, 1831; Huldah, June 24, 1834, died Oct. 1, 1841; Joseph O., Oct. 14,

1840. Albina mar. Samuel F. Bartlett of Cummington, (second wife) Dec. 7, 1865.—Joseph O. mar. Lucy L. Allen of Windsor, Dec. 24, 1867. Children: Edwin S., born Nov. 11, 1869; Alida L., Aug. 14, 1871, died in infancy; Lucy A., Dec. 8, 1875; Joseph A., Oct. 28, 1877; Mary A., July 7, 1879; Albert O., July 16, 1887.—Edwin S. mar. Emma A. Gardner, Nov. 16, 1890.

6. Bethuel mar. Sarah Stockwell, Dec. 8, 1831. Had one son, Levi W., born Feb. 28, 1833. Married Mary J. Stowell of Hinsdale, Mass., Sept. 15, 1869. No children. Was chosen one of the Selectmen in 1883, and served five years. Sarah, wife of Bethuel, died Nov. 12, 1851. For a second wife he married Mrs. Julia A. M. Joy, widow of Charles Joy, May 6, 1852. They reside on the homestead where his father Joseph lived.

MOSES HALLOCK.

Rev. Moses Hallock was a grandson of Noah Hallock, born 1696, and died 1773. His son William was born 1730, and died Oct. 21, 1815. He had two sons, Jeremiah and Moses, and at least six daughters, one of whom, Esther, married Rev. Josiah Hayden, and was the mother of Josiah Jr. and Hon. Joel Hayden of Williamsburg, Mass. Moses was born in Brookhaven, L. I., Feb. 16, 1760. Installed over the Plainfield church in 1792. Married Margaret Allen, who was born at Chilmark, Martha's Vineyard, March 22, 1760, and died Dec. 29, 1835. The following is an extract from a letter from Mr. Hallock to his absent sons, informing them of the death of their mother: "Plainfield, Dec. 30, 1835. My dear sons and daughters: Yesterday, about half-past eleven, your mother died. But it seemed more like quiet sleep than death. A fortnight

ago to-day she suddenly became speechless and helpless. Martha and I laid her on the bed. Dr. Shaw came very soon, and said it was a shock of paralysis. He visited her daily, and Mrs. Arnold Streeter and Mrs. Salem Streeter kindly assisted day and night in the care of her till she died. She had her reason almost or quite till the last."
A short time before his death he committed to the flames all his manuscripts except a few which he might still wish to use; and when his only daughter, who was the solace of his declining years, seconding the desire of her brothers, requested that he would prepare at least an outline of the facts of his history, he replied, "No, Martha; the absent sons might wish to see it, but there is nothing remarkable about me." He died most peacefully, as befitted his peaceful life, on the evening of July 17, 1837. On the second day after his death, his funeral took place, the sermon being preached by Rev. Dr. Theophilus Packard of Shelburne. Of the bereaved church, *only one* who was a member at the time of his installation, survived him, the venerable Deacon James Richards. As the face of the aged pastor was uncovered that the people might approach and take their final leave until the resurrection, the aged deacon, now entirely blind, was led to the coffin, placed his hand gently on the forehead of him with whom he had for forty-five years shared the burden and heat of the gospel day, and stood, pouring out a flood of tears, till constrained to retire, he turned away, saying, "Farewell for time." Mention has already been made of the classical school taught by Mr. Hallock in his dwelling-house in Chap. IV of this work. In the records of Williams College it is said that for a long time in the early struggles of that institution, the question of how many students were to enter

at the beginning of each college year depended in a great measure upon the number Mr. Hallock could furnish. Half the class were not infrequently from his school. The cost of board and tuition in this institution was one dollar per week. Mrs. Martha J. Lamb, the eminent historian, is our authority for these statements. It is a well authenticated fact that John Brown of Harper's Ferry notoriety was at one time a member of this school. Tradition says that his ancestors lived in the neighboring town of Savoy. The children of Moses Hallock were William A., born June 2, 1794; Martha, Feb. 24, 1796; Leavitt, Jan. 21, 1798; Gerard, March 18, 1800, and Homan.

1. William A. graduated at Williams in 1819, studied divinity at Andover and while there was chosen agent, and afterwards assistant secretary of the American Tract Society, then located at Andover. Assisted in the formation of the same society at New York in 1825, and was chosen the first corresponding secretary and general agent. He held the office of secretary until his death, which occurred some ten years since. He married Fanny Lathrop and had two daughters, Harriet and Frances.

2. Martha never married. Died in Plainfield, May 22, 1852.

3. Leavitt settled in town, and married Elizabeth Snell of Cummington, Aug., 1829. At this time, persons intending marriage, must, according to law, be "cried;" that is, they must notify the town clerk of their intention at least three weeks previous to the intended marriage. It was then his duty to enter the same on the records, and each Sabbath afterward, for three weeks in succession, when the people were assembled at church, just before the opening of service, he arose and gravely announced the same

to the congregation. The year of Leavitt's marriage he was himself town clerk, and it became his embarrassing duty to "cry" himself. He proved himself however equal to the occasion, and when the Sabbath arrived and the people were assembled, stood up and bravely announced, "Marriage intended, between Leavitt Hallock of Plainfield and Elizabeth Snell of Cummington." He served as town clerk two years, was commissioned a Justice of the Peace in 1834, and represented the town in the Legislature in 1849. He was also for some years Postmaster. He was a very energetic man, of great business capacity. He utilized the water privilege and established the settlement just over Plainfield line in the town of Hawley, which still bears his name. He erected several dams, commencing about 1836, and established a large tannery there, sawmills, &c. He also erected and operated a store and boarding-house, doing a successful business until 1846, when the tannery was burned, Feb. 11. This was rebuilt in 1848 but never operated and the place in a few years went to decay. He was instrumental in obtaining the laying out and construction of several important new roads. He was a very persistent man, not easily daunted by obstacles, and rarely failed in what he undertook. He erected the house and outbuildings and made many handsome improvements on the place lately owned by Dea. J. Barber, which he then owned and occupied. About 1854 he removed to Amherst, Mass., where he did quite a business in real estate. He died at the home of his son, Leavitt H., in West Winsted, Conn., Oct. 16, 1875. His wife died Dec. 19, 1877, aged 74. Children: Fanny and Eliza, twins, born May 12, 1830; William A., Aug. 27, 1832 ; Sarah, May 3, 1836, died Feb. 16, 1837;

LEAVITT HALLOCK.
AT 60.

Moses, born Nov., 1839, died Sept. 3, 1846; Leavitt H., Aug. 15, 1842.—Fanny mar. Rev. Henry M. Hazeltine about 1855.—Eliza mar. Thos. H. Rouse of Windsor, Conn., Sept. 16, 1851.

William A. entered the ministry. Was pastor of the church in Gilead, Conn. Afterwards preached in Kiantone and other places in Chautauqua Co., N. Y. For twelve years, from 1875 to 1887, had charge of the Cong. Church in Bloomfield, Conn. He married Clara M. Hall of Jamestown, N. Y., Sept. 19, 1860. Children: Nellie E., lately graduated at Smith College, Northampton, and William Hall, a graduate of Amherst College; at present a member of Berlin University, Berlin, Germany.

Leavitt H. also entered the ministry. Was for eleven years pastor of the Cong. Church at West Winsted, Conn. Six years pastor at Portland, Maine. Now pastor of the First Cong. Church at Waterville, Me. Married Martie B. Butler of Brooklyn, N. Y., June 11, 1867. She died Oct. 2, 1873. Children: Lillian H. and Harry Butler. Lillian studied at Wellesley College and is now teaching High School at Hallowell, Me. Harry is in class of '93 at Amherst College.—Leavitt H. married for a second wife Nellie M. Webster of Portland, Oct. 3, 1888.

4. Gerard graduated at Williams College in 1819. Engaged in teaching for awhile but soon went to Boston and started a newspaper called the "Boston Telegraph." This after one year was merged in the Boston Recorder. He continued to edit the united papers until 1826, when he sold out his interest to Rev. Asa Rand, and removed to N. Y. city, where he became one of the editors and proprietors of the N. Y. Observer. He afterwards became editor and proprietor of the Journal of Commerce, which he con-

ducted ably for nearly forty years. Later, having removed his residence to New Haven, Conn., he paid nearly $30,000 out of a total expense of $35,000 incurred in building the South Cong. Church and chapel in that city.—He married Eliza Allen of Chilmark. Deceased Jan. 4, 1866. Had two sons, Wm. Holmes, born Aug. 18, 1826, and Charles, March 13, 1834.—Wm. H. mar. Julia Mack of Plainfield, Sept. 3, 1851. Is at present assistant editor of the "Iron Age." Both sons were connected with the Journal of Commerce for many years in an editorial capacity. Charles was connected with The "Forest and Stream" as editor from 1873 to 1880, and is the author of a number of valuable works, among which are the following: "Fishing Tourist," published in 1873; "Camp Life in Florida," 1876; "Sportsman's Gazetteer," 1877; "Vacation Rambles in Michigan," 1877; "Our New Alaska," a very interesting work, 1886; "Salmon Fisher," 1890. He married Amelia J. Wardell of Newark, N. J. Visits Plainfield nearly every summer, usually remaining several weeks. He was the founder of the town of Hallock, county-seat of Kittson county, Minnesota, at present the most flourishing locality in the Red River Valley. His portrait was received too late to be indexed.

5. Homan, youngest son of Moses, in 1826 went as a missionary printer to the island of Malta, in the Mediterranean, and some years after to Smyrna. When the American Bible Society commenced the publication of the Arabic Bible in New York, it is said that only two persons in the world understood the manufacture of the Arabic type. These were an aged German and Homan Hallock. About this time he returned to Plainfield where with the assistance of his son Samuel he carried on the manufacture of

CHARLES HALLOCK.

the Arabic type. When after a few years the work was transferred to Beyrout, Syria, Samuel went there also and took the position which his father had occupied, and is still engaged in that work.

Homan, in the course of his travels, became acquainted with and married an English lady, Mrs. Elizabeth Johnson, a most estimable woman, who deceased Sept. 18, 1875, aged seventy-six. They had five sons, Moses, Homan B., Gerard J., Samuel and Wm. A., and two daughters, Margaret and Sarah. Margaret married Rev. T. L. Byington, May 30, 1858, and for more than twenty years they were missionaries among the Bulgarians and at Constantinople. Sarah married Chas. C. Streeter, May 11, 1859. They reside in Cummington. Her father, aged nearly ninety, makes his home with them.

JOHN HAMLEN.

[The writer has been able by referring to the printed record of the Hamlen family, compiled by the late Dea. Freeman Hamlen, and kindly loaned for the purpose by his widow, Mrs. Martha Hamlen, to prepare a more complete history of this family than of any other which he has attempted.]

The Hamlens are of French origin; they came to England about 1080. James Hamblen[1] and his wife Anne emigrated to this country in 1640, and settled in Barnstable, Mass. He died in 1690.

John[2], son of James[1], born in Barnstable, June 30, 1644, married Sarah Bearse, August, 1667.

Benjamin[3], son of John[2] and Sarah, born in Barnstable, Feb. 11, 1686, settled in Eastham, Mass., in 1716; married for his second wife, Anna Mayo, great grand-daughter of Gov. Prince.

Isaac[4], son of Benjamin[3] and Anna, born in 1728; married Sarah Shaw of Abington.

John[5], son of Isaac[4] and Sarah, born in Bridgewater, Mass., Oct. 22, 1762; married Sally Towne.

The name of Hamlen has been variously written: often Ham*blen*, and as often Ham*lin* and Ham*len*.

In the year 1776, John Hamlen, then thirteen years old, removed with his parents to Cummington, three years before its incorporation as a town. At the age of sixteen he entered the Revolutionary army and served about six months. He was at the time of his death the last of the Revolutionary pensioners in Plainfield. He married Sally Town (born in Sutton, Mass.) at Windsor, Mass., 1790, and settled in Plainfield the same year. He was by trade a carpenter and several of the first houses were built by him or under his supervision. The house which he built and occupied on his homestead where E. A. Atkins now lives, is still in good condition. In 1800 he was chosen one of the selectmen and served for nineteen years. He represented the town in General Court at Boston in 1813, '14 and '15; also in 1823 and 1826. He made the journey to Boston on horseback, and during the May sessions turned his horse out to pasture in the near vicinity, and at the end of the session rode home again. Two other representatives were at the time of their election living in the John Hamlen house, viz.: his son Freeman and Edwin A. Atkins, the present member from this town. His wife died Oct. 11, 1818, aged forty-five. For a second wife he married Mrs. Dorothy Gove of Worthington, Nov. 10, 1819. She died Sept. 21, 1847, aged sixty-nine. Although for many years in feeble health he lacked but a few months of being ninety years of age at his death, which occurred April 15, 1852. At the age of seventy-five he publicly professed his faith in Christ as a Savior, and united with the Plainfield church. He had

JOHN HAMLEN.

however for some years previously entertained a Christian hope. Children of John and Sally Hamlen were John, Jr., born July 29, 1791, died Feb. 20, 1792; Orren, born Dec. 2, 1792; Reuben, May 19, 1795; Clarissa, July 5, 1797; Nabby, Feb. 10, 1800; Lyman, Jan. 14, 1803; Freeman, May 8, 1805; Polly, Sept. 15, 1807; Horace, Aug. 23, 1810; John, Jr., (2d) Dec. 3, 1814.

2. Orren died Sept. 14, 1813.

3. Reuben settled in Plainfield and was five times married. His first wife was Rhoda Richards. Married Feb. 15, 1816, died Dec. 29, 1826.—Second, Fanny Warner, mar. April 17, 1828, died July 22, 1839.—Third, Elizabeth Jones, mar. Nov. 3, 1839, died Dec. 11, 1851.—Fourth, Mrs. Eunice, widow of Abram S. Tirrell, mar. Jan. 1, 1854, died Jan. 1, 1864.—Fifth, Mrs. Pamela Little of Shelburne Falls, mar. Sept. 23, 1866. She survived him. He died at Shelburne Falls, Mass., Dec. 28, 1866. Children of Reuben and Rhoda were Marilla R., born June 4, 1817, died Oct. 7, 1837; Flora A., March 29, 1819, died June 12, 1840; Martha A., March 28, 1821; Shepard L., Feb. 14, 1823; Laura B., April, 1825, died Oct. 14, 1826. Children of Reuben and Fanny W. were Laura B., born April 27, 1829; Rosamond W., June 1, 1831, died Aug. 29, 1844; Alfred W., June 17, 1834; Albert Wallace, March 13, 1839.—Martha A. mar. Wm. C. Bissell of Twinsburg, O., March 19, 1855, died Sept. 8, 1857.—Shepard L. mar. Elizabeth B. Valentine of Cincinnati, Nov. 19, 1850, died May 6, 1866.—Laura B. mar. James C. Bellman of Cincinnati, Dec. 22, 1853.—Alfred W. mar. Harriet N. Stratton of Jeffersonville, Ind., Nov. 19, 1863, died June 6, 1872.—Albert Wallace mar. Rachel Mercer of Princeton, Ill., Oct. 27, 1870.—None of Reuben's children settled in Plainfield.

4. Clarissa mar. Otis Pratt, Jan. 18, 1817, died Dec. 13, 1831.

5. Nabby mar. John Ford of Cummington, Sept. 3, 1818; died Sept. 29, 1833.

6. Lyman mar. Lucy Flint of West Bloomfield, N. Y., 1826. Children: Sarah E., born May 20, 1827; Mary M., April 3, 1830; Amelia, March 29, 1833; Horace, June 8, 1835, died Feb. 8, 1839; Horatio B., Aug. 1, 1837; William V., Aug. 29, 1840; Martha A., Feb. 2, 1843; Alice Flora, June 25, 1846, died Jan. 25, 1854; Edwin C., Jan. 11, 1849, died Nov. 14, 1865; Frederick B., July 31, 1853.—Sarah E. mar. John C. Johns of West Bloomfield, N. Y., Sept. 7, 1848.—Mary M. mar. Russell Bradley, Nov. 13, 1854.— Amelia mar. Wm. D. Quick, March 29, 1854.—Horatio B. mar. Harriet Brown of Clarkston, Mich., Dec. 17, 1861. —Martha A. mar. Dennis Collins of Clarkston, Mich., May 2, 1865.—Frederick B. mar. Lizzie Weeks of Pontiac, Mich.

7. Freeman mar. Clarissa Whiting, June 4, 1829. She deceased Oct. 13, 1847. For a second wife he married Martha Taylor of Hawley, Nov. 30, 1848. Was chosen one of the Selectmen in 1846 and served six years. Represented the town in the Legislature in 1850 and 1851. In 1853 he was chosen town clerk, an office which he held for twenty-three years in succession, at the end of which time he declined further service. During his term of service he indexed all the town records of births, marriages, deaths and intentions of marriage, which had not been done previous to 1864, adding many that had been omitted, particularly births, thus rendering the records of far greater value. For this labor he asked no compensation. Was chosen deacon of the Congregational church Aug. 30, 1844, serving most acceptably until his resignation in 1867. He was also

for many years clerk of the church and compiled the last church manual published in 1884. He and his brother Reuben were for many years leaders of the church choir, both having excellent voices. Freeman remained on the old homestead until about 1855, when he removed to the village. He died on the morning of Jan. 16, 1889, while seated in the family sitting room. He had been in feeble health for some time, and his death, though sudden, was not wholly unexpected. He was a man of thorough honesty and sound judgment, and was worthy of and received the confidence of the entire community. Humility, sincerity and charity were marked features of his Christian character. Truly, in many ways, "he being dead yet speaketh." He had one child only, a son by his first wife, Edward F, born June 6, 1842. He served as first Sergeant in Co. I 52d Mass. in the war for the Union. Was for a number of years after his return from the army in business in Northampton. Is now employed at the State House, Boston, as Executive Clerk for the Governor and Council, a position which he has held for some fifteen years. He married Helen A. Church of N. Y. City, June 9, 1868. Franklin Church, son of Edward F. and Helen A., was born in Boston, Sept. 19, 1876.

8. Polly mar. Mason Ames, May 12, 1830, died in Chester, Ohio, March 18, 1847.

9. Horace mar. Clarissa Bancroft of Granville, Ohio, May 1, 1834. She deceased Aug. 8, 1875. For a second wife he mar. Mrs. Lizzie Gavnen of Gratiot, Ohio, July 6, 1876. One son, Samuel B., born Feb. 20, 1835, mar. Lydia Clark of Easthampton, Mass., Sept. 16, 1856.

10. John Jr. (2d) died in Granville, Ohio, Oct. 22, 1844.

JACOB JONES.

Jacob Jones, son of John and Ruth, was born in Weymouth, Mass., Nov. 1770. His father died in 1800 and his mother in 1814, aged seventy-four. He mar. Elizabeth Whiton, sister of Maj. David Whiton, Nov. 27, 1800. They lived on the farm now occupied by his grandson, William Jones. Died Aug. 22, 1861. Children: Addison, born 1801, died Oct. 4. 1832; Jacob Jr., born July 9, 1802; Merritt, Feb. 19, 1804; Elizabeth, Dec. 25, 1805; Nancy, Aug. 29, 1807; Sarah, April 22, 1809; Minerva, July 15, 1811; Hannah, Feb. 3, 1815.

2. Jacob Jr. mar. Lucy H. Howes of Ashfield, March, 1828. Died suddenly while at work Dec. 15, 1873. Children: Mary Christina, born July 28, 1829; William, May 13, 1832; Nancy W., June 1, 1834; David, July 20, 1838, died June 18, 1845; Samuel W., born Aug. 26, 1842.—M. Christina mar. Ansel K. Bradford, Sept. 27, 1849. Reside in Florence, Mass.—William mar. Caroline M. Field of Windsor, Mass., March, 1856. One daughter, Anna M., born Oct. 9, 1868, mar. Frederic M. Rice of Ashfield, April 13, 1887.—Nancy W. mar. Seth W. Clark, Sept. 3, 1855.—Samuel W. served in the civil war in the 46th Mass. After his return from the army he removed to Lockport, Ill., where he mar. Eliza Paddock, Dec. 25, 1867. Children: Hattie, born Oct. 9, 1868, since deceased, and William, born 1872.

3. Merritt mar. Celia Gardner, June 30, 1825. She died May 22, 1845. For a second wife he mar. Mrs. Chloe R. K. Ford, widow of William Ford, July 26, 1846. Served as one of the Selectmen in 1863, died Dec. 30, 1884. Children by his first wife, Rozelia M., born Aug. 31, 1830,

died July 24, 1840; Sarah A., born Feb. 22, 1842, died Oct. 7, 1857; also two others who died in infancy.
4. Elizabeth mar. Reuben Hamlen, (third wife) Nov. 3, 1839, died Dec. 11, 1851.
5. Nancy mar. Seth S. Williams of Ashfield, Oct. 5, 1826, and is the only surviving member of this family.
6. Sarah mar. Samuel Williams of Ashfield, Oct. 24, 1833.
7. Minerva mar. Chester Clark, Dec. 1, 1831, died July 22, 1885.
8. Hannah mar. John Clark, Dec., 1834.

ISAAC JOY.

Isaac Joy was a pioneer settler from Weymouth, Mass. Lived a short distance south of where W. E. Shaw now lives. He had the honor of serving the warrant calling the first district meeting, it being directed to him as a "principle inhabitant." Was chosen one of the Selectmen in 1788, serving two years. His wife, Hannah, died March 4, 1797. For a second wife mar. Mrs. Hannah Hathaway of Adams, Oct., 1799. Died July 20, 1801. Children: Isaac, Jr., born 1761; Joseph, 1763; Mary, who mar. Ezekiel Eldred, and Hannah, who mar. John Taylor of Hawley, Nov. 22, 1810. All these children were born in Weymouth, Mass.—Isaac, Jr., mar. Ruth Tirrell, Dec., 1785, died March 5, 1843. Children: William, born Dec. 23, 1786; Zenas, Jan. 20, 1790; Lucinda, Nov. 29, 1796; Alonzo, May 17, 1801; Susanna, (known as Susan) Feb. 27, 1803; Harriet, Nov. 2, 1804; Isaac, (3d) June 9, 1815, and one who died in infancy. It is remarkable that there was a difference of nearly twenty-eight and one-half years in the ages of the oldest and youngest of this family.

1. William mar. Sally Campbell, March, 1810. Children: Fordyce, born Sept. 19, 1811; Lydia, Feb. 4, 1814; Horace, Feb. 23, 1816; Rozina, May 22, 1818; William, Jr., Feb. 23, 1821; Edwin, June 7, 1823.

2. Zenas mar. Abigail Everett of Northampton. The birth of one child only appears on the records, Lewis, born Jan. 25, 1812.

3. Lucinda mar. Quartus Taylor.

4. Alonzo mar. Lois Kingman of Hawley. Children: James T., Horatio and Julia A. His wife deceased, and for a second he mar. Minerva Smith of Hawley. Children: Caroline A., born Oct. 28, 1846, died Oct. 13, 1850; Emily, born Sept. 20, 1848, died Sept. 2, 1850; William F., born April 6, 1853.—James T. mar. Mary J. Taylor, Feb. 24, 1853.—Julia A. mar. C. Thayer of Hadley.

5. Susan mar. James Cook, Jan. 24, 1833.

6. Harriet mar. Abishur Nash, Jan. 11, 1827.

7. Isaac (3d) removed to Cambridgeport, Mass., where he married and now resides.

Joseph Joy, son of Isaac 1st, mar. Molly Porter of Abington. She died Jan 19, 1826, aged sixty-five. For a second wife he mar. Mrs. Mehitable Brown of Abington, Sept. 1829. She died March 15, 1836, aged sixty-seven. He died Nov. 22, 1839. His children were Clarissa, born Feb. 21, 1788; Leonard, March 14, 1790; James, Sept. 1, 1793; Polly, May 10, 1796; Merilla, Aug. 20, 1800; Electa, Feb. 11, 1803; and one who died in infancy.

1. Clarissa mar. Levi Campbell, June 14, 1810, died Dec. 26, 1856.

2. Leonard mar. Polly Warner, daughter of Abel, Nov. 19, 1811. Died Jan. 15, 1881. For some years kept the

hotel known as the "Hampshire House." Children : Lucretia, born Aug 19, 1813, died March 17, 1818; Cordelia, born May 27, 1815; Sarah M., March 28, 1817; Emeline and Caroline, (twins) June 15, 1819; Francis W., May 13, 1822; Charles, Oct. 16, 1824; Electa P., 1827; Lorenzo W., born in Worthington, 1832.—Cordelia mar. Rush Gurney of Cummington, second wife, about 1839.—Sarah M. mar. John M. Crane of Washington, Mass., Sept. 19, 1838. —Caroline mar. Jonas Holden of Hawley, May 10, 1841.— Francis W. mar. Rachel Chapel of Washington, Mass., April, 1845, died Aug. 17, 1887.—Charles mar. Julia M. Sanderson, Nov., 1848, died Aug. 12, 1850.—Electa P. mar. Reuben Scott, Jr., of Hawley, June 3, 1847.—Lorenzo W. mar. Delia R. Colburn, Jan., 1855.

3. James mar. Mary Whiton, June 10, 1818. Children: Mary Ann P., born June 23, 1819; Amelia Antoinette, Nov. 2, 1823; Clara H., May 30, 1830. Mary Ann mar. Elisha Bassett, now Clerk of the U. S. District Court at Boston, Sept. 5, 1843.—Antoinette mar. William Bassett, April 2, 1845. They reside in Heath, Mass.—Clara H. mar. Benj. F. Hallett of Boston, (second wife) Aug. 4, 1858. He was the senior member of the Hallett & Davis Piano Company, and deceased several years since. Mrs. Hallett now resides in Florence, Mass.

4. Polly mar. Verus Patrick, March 27, 1822.
5. Merilla mar. Dura Torrey, Dec. 4, 1821.
6. Electa mar. Levi Clark, Oct. 2, 1828, both of whom are still living in town.

JACOB NASH.

Jacob Nash was born in Weymouth, Mass., in 1760. Served through the entire war of the Revolution, although at the beginning only fifteen years of age, and came to

Plainfield directly after the close of the war and settled on the farm now occupied by Stephen Parsons. In 1788 he mar. Joan Reade of Abington, whose English ancestors came to America in the Mayflower. She died Sept. 8, 1849, aged eighty-six. He died April 14, 1851. Their children were Sybil, born Aug. 19, 1789; Arvin, Nov. 19, 1790; Roxana, Aug. 22, 1792, died Jan. 20, 1868; Eunice, April 30, 1795; Mandana, Jan. 19, 1800. Sybil and Roxana never married.—Arvin mar. Lucinda Vinton in 1813. Children : Eunice V., Martha J., Spencer and Maria S. Eunice and Spencer died in childhood.

Martha J. mar. Chas. A. Lamb, Sept. 8, 1852. She has since become well known in the literary world. Among her notable productions are "The History of the City of New York," in two folio volumes, considered in many respects the most remarkable city history ever written; "The Homes of America," published by the Appletons in 1879; "Memorial of Dr. J. D. Russ;" "Wall Street in History," thirteen volumes for children, which have gone through many editions; "Spicy," a novel, celebrated for containing the best description extant of the great Chicago fire; her work on the coast survey used as a text book in some of our colleges, and upwards of one hundred and fifty important historical and other papers in leading magazines. Early in 1883 Mrs. Lamb was made editor-in-chief of the "Magazine of American History," a position she still holds (1891.) It has won the distinction of being one of the best edited and best conducted magazines of its kind in the world, and is in all the first-class public libraries of the English speaking cities of three continents, a valued authority in all leading literary circles. Mrs. Lamb's work is of the highest character and is recognized as such among the most eminent scholars in all parts of the world. She has been elected to membership in twenty-six historical and learned societies in this country and Europe,—honors never before conferred on any American woman. Her residence for the past twenty-five years has been in New York City.

Maria S. mar. J. S. Whitmarsh, (second wife) April 10, 1865. Reside in Florence, Mass.

Arvin's wife having deceased he mar. for a second Mrs. Dorothy Covell of Buckland. Children : James A. and Mary L.—James A. mar. Mary A. Torrey, Sept. 16, 1860. He settled in town and has been for about twenty-five years proprietor of the grist-mill standing near the site of the old mill formerly owned by Dea. Joseph Beals, "the Mountain Miller." Was chosen one of the Selectmen in 1874, and served nine years, a part of the time as chairman. Children : Elmer E., born in Chicago; Frank E., born July 25, 1866; Charles A., Aug. 14, 1870 ; Lewis S., Sept. 20, 1884.—Mary L. mar. John Baker of Savoy. He recently deceased in Adams, Mass., where his widow still resides.—Arvin Nash's second wife died in 1841, and he mar. Lucretia Pixley, Sept. 20, 1842. He died July 12, 1869.—Eunice, daughter of Jacob, mar. David Crittenden of Charlemont, Sept. 1, 1813.—Mandana, daughter of Jacob, mar. Jacob Pratt, May 29, 1828, and is now living in South Amherst, Mass., at the advanced age of 91.

BARNABAS PACKARD.

Barnabas Packard was born in Cummington in 1764, his father's name being also Barnabas. He mar. Mary Nash of Plainfield, July, 1789, and settled on the farm where Thos. K. Wheeler lives, south of Orrin Tirrell's, died April 30, 1847. Children : Achsah, born April 26, 1790, died June 21, 1791; Sally, born July 3, 1792, died April 25, 1868, unmarried; Barnabas, Jr., born June 10, 1795; Patty, Aug. 25, 1797; Ruby, Sept. 29, 1799; Norton, Nov. 22, 1802 ; Milton, Jan. 10, 1805 ; Roswell, Feb. 15, 1808, and one who died in infancy June 14, 1794.

Barnabas, Jr. mar. Ruth Snow, died at Cameron, Mo., in 1872. Children : Polly N., born July 18, 1819, died Nov. 10, 1868, unmarried ; Cynthia, born Nov. 27, 1820 ; Wm. H., Oct. 1, 1822 ; Patty (or Martha) Aug. 18, 1824; Irene, Sept. 20, 1826 ; Mary Jane, Oct. 22, 1828 ; Roswell Clifford, Feb. 4, 1831 ; Chalmer O., July, 1834 ; Charles Edwin, March 19, 1838; H. Clark, Feb. 20, 1840.

Cynthia mar. Aaron G. Ayres, Dec., 1841.

William H. mar. Rachel B. Tillson of Cummington, April, 1847, and settled in Windsor. Children: Cornelia, Joseph, Tillson, Luther W., Cyrus W., B. Franklin, Fred, Mary and Henry C. Rachel, wife of Wm. H., died Jan. 30, 1881. For a second wife he mar. Mrs. Mary Ann (Dyer) Brackett, Oct. 26, 1887. Of the children of Wm. H., Cornelia, Joseph and Tillson (deceased) settled in Canada.—Luther mar. Lucy O. Stetson, Oct. 18, 1882. Children : Minnie R., Annie E. and Mary E.—Cyrus W. mar. Nellie Mason, April 14, 1878. She deceased, and for a second wife he mar. Dora A. Mills. Their children are John H., Maggie A., Joseph W., Charles, Marion E. and Robert B.—B. Franklin mar. Julia E. Beals, of Goshen, June 25, 1890, one son, Joseph A. Fred died Aug. 12, 1884, aged twenty-four. Mary died July 13, 1887, aged twenty-five.—Henry C. mar. Bertha B. Gurney, Dec. 14, 1890.—Martha, daughter of Barnabas, Jr., mar. Charles

T. Ford of Windsor, Dec., 1843.—Irene mar. Horatio Lyon, April, 1847.—Mary Jane mar. Zebedee H. Randall of Cummington, March, 1852.—Clifford mar. Elnora J. Vining of Cummington, Feb. 25, 1869, and settled in Missouri. Children : Emma E., born March 9, 1870 ; Geo. C., March 13, 1873 ; Leonard C., Dec. 8, 1875; Etta B., Dec. 13, 1877; E. Edwin, Feb. 1, 1880; Jennie S., Aug. 5, 1882.—Chalmer mar. Sophia Dean of Savoy, April 1, 1863 ; settled in Missouri. Have one son, Herbert M., born July, 1867.—Chas. Edwin mar. Araminta Utter of Ohio in 1867, settled in Missouri. Children : Wm. B., born Sept. 19, 1870; Clark S., Dec. 29, 1873; Eva L., Aug. 10, 1876 ; Martha P., Feb. 5, 1880 ; Bessie D., 1884 ; Laura E., Aug. 10, 1886, and an infant daughter who died in 1870. —These three brothers all reside at Cameron, Mo., Edwin being cashier of the Farmers' Bank at that place.—H. Clark mar. Melona C. Dawes, June 4, 1865. One daughter, Vesta D., born Aug. 28, 1866, mar. Arthur B. Richards of Cummington, June 29, 1890.

Patty, daughter of Barnabas, mar. Nathan Beals, July 13, 1815.

Norton, son of Barnabas, mar. Mary Ann Thompson, 1828. Children : George W., born Jan. 30, 1829 ; Philena M., Nov. 27, 1834 ; Marilla B., April 25, 1837 ; John K., Aug. 16, 1839.

Milton, son of Barnabas, mar. Charlotte Parker, Jan. 7, 1828. Children : Lurinda, born Aug. 30, 1830 ; Lyman, April 15, 1833 ; Leavitt, Oct. 19. 1835 ; Laura, Jan. 23, 1843; Lozene E., Jan. 18, 1845 ; Franklin, Dec. 12, 1852; Lyman and Leavitt went West and died there.—Lozene mar. Mina Wheeler. They reside in Windsor. Have several children.—Franklin mar. Nellie Whitman. Reside in Cummington and have quite a family.

Roswell, son of Barnabas, mar. Susan Bird of Williamstown, July, 1832. They had one daughter born in Plainfield, Vesta, Oct. 9, 1833.

JAMES RICHARDS.

James Richards was the son of Joseph and Sarah (Whitmarsh) Richards, the fourth of a family of four sons and three daughters. He was born in Eastern Massachusetts, May 31, 1757. Was one of the earliest settlers and had seen service in the Revolutionary army. He was an educated man, of versatile talents, and throughout his active life was prominent in church and town affairs. Was one of the first two deacons chosen Nov. 15, 1792. Taught school in winter for many years. Was a fine singer and organized and led the first choir; also taught singing schools in early times in this and adjoining towns. He was held in high esteem by the towns-people. and his opinion on any public question had the effect of law. One Sunday morning a new minister had preached, and as the congregation were passing out one asked another how he liked the sermon, "Oh, I don't know," he replied, "I haven't seen Deacon Richards yet." He was chosen one of the Selectmen in 1790 and served in that capacity twenty-one years. Only one has served the town in that office longer, the exception being Levi N. Campbell, who served twenty-two years. In 1797 he was chosen Town Clerk and served four years. Represented the District and Cummington in General Court in 1793, '98, and 1801, 3 and 5, and after its incorporation as a town he was sent as its representative in 1811, '12 and '16. He was also a delegate to the Convention for Revising the Constitution in Nov., 1820. Was commissioned a Justice of the Peace in 1802, an office at that time attended with far greater responsibilities than now, which office he held twenty-eight years. He was totally blind for some years previous to his death, which occurred Mch. 1, 1842. Mar. Lydia Shaw of Abington, sister of Josiah Shaw, May 1, 1780. She died Aug. 20, 1828, aged seventy-one. She is spoken of by those who remember her as a most excellent woman. The homestead on which they settled and where they lived and died is that now occupied by A. B. Cole, the house now standing being the same occupied by them. This was built before 1800, probably, and was the birth-place of the writer. Their children were a daughter, born May 1, 1781, who died in infancy; Lydia, born May 1, 1782; James, Jr., Feb. 23, 1784; Joseph, Nov. 6, 1785; Sarah, Aug. 15, 1787; Nancy Shaw, Jan. 5, 1790, died Dec. 20, 1794; William, Aug. 22, 1793; Jason, June 27, 1796, died May 1, 1798; Jason (2d) Aug. 31, 1798; Austin, Feb. 9, 1800. Of these, the first five were born before their settlement in Plainfield.—Lydia mar. Ebenezer Snell, Esq., of Cummington, (second wife) Oct. 27, 1825, died June 26, 1846.

James, Jr. graduated at Williams College in 1809. Studied theology at Andover, graduating in 1812. While at college he with four others, of whom Samuel J. Mills was the leader, became greatly interested in the subject of foreign missions and prayed into existence the American Board of Commissioners for Foreign Missions. In September, 1811, he offered his services to the Board as a missionary. After completing his theological studies he devoted considerable time to the study of medicine and surgery, with a view to increased usefulness among the heathen. He mar. Sarah Bardwell, May 31, 1815, and Oct. 23, 1815, they sailed for Ceylon, where they arrived after a voyage, considered a prosperous one, but which required *five months*. After over six years of faithful labor, part of which time, however, Mr. Richards was greatly hindered by sickness, he died at Tillapilly, Ceylon, Aug. 3, 1822. A monument bearing suitable inscriptions in English and Tamul, marks his last resting place. His widow died April 26, 1825.

Joseph mar. Mehitable Allen, April 4, 1809. He was a physician and located at Hillsdale, N. Y. Had one son, William, also a physician, for several years located in Cummington. Married Martha Brown of Peru.

Sarah mar. John Mack, Oct. 27, 1808, died Jan. 25, 1866.

William studied for the ministry, graduated at Williams College in 1819, studied divinity at Andover, offered his services as a missionary, and was ordained at New Haven, Sept. 12, 1822. He mar. Clarissa Lyman, and they sailed for the Sandwich Islands, Nov. 19, 1822, arriving there in April, 1823. He became an influential adviser of the King of the islands, and after fifteen years at the work of civilizing and christianizing the people and aiding in translating the Bible into their language, he entered the service of their government and gave shape and direction to their politics. His first duty was to prepare a constitution and code of laws for the nation, which remains, a lasting monument to his memory. He then sailed for Europe and the United States as Minister Plenipotentiary of the King, to obtain from the great powers of the earth an acknowledgment of the Sandwich Islands as an independent kingdom. His credentials, handsomely engrossed on vellum, bearing the signature and seal of the king, are now in the possession of his neice, Mrs. Wm. Holmes Hallock.

Mr. Richards was accompanied to the United States by Prince Haalilio, the heir apparent to the Hawaiian throne, whose visit to Plainfield will be remembered by a few. The prince died at sea on the return passage. After Mr. Richards' return to the Sandwich Islands, he was for several years Minister of Public Instruction, and his labors were incessant. The king had perfect confidence in his judgment and considered him his best friend. His death, which occurred Nov. 7, 1847, was by them regarded as a national bereavement.

Jason received as thorough an education as could be obtained at the common schools. He spent his life in Plainfield and cared for his parents until their death. He taught very successfully for many years in the schools of this and adjacent towns. Was chosen Town Clerk in 1833 and held the office twelve years. He was a very plain and careful penman and very exact in making records. He represented the town in the Legislature in 1841 and '42. About this time he was appointed a Justice of the Peace, an office which he held until a short time before his death, which occurred Aug. 7, 1885. It is somewhat remarkable that he professed Christ and united with the church at the advanced age of seventy-eight years, giving good evidence during the remainder of his life that he had indeed "passed from death unto life." He gave much attention to the study of common law and though he never took any regular course, was considered excellent authority by the people of the town in ordinary matters of law, being often consulted on legal subjects, and his opinions when given were very seldom wrong. Had he received a thorough legal education he would without doubt have been a shining light in that profession, for which he had great natural talents. He mar. Sophia Forsaith of Deering, N. H., Jan. 5, 1830. Children: Ann S., born Oct. 22, 1830; James Forsaith, July 16, 1832; William Austin, Jan. 27, 1836; Laura Mack, July 18, 1838.

James F. received a college education, studied medicine and is a successful physician in Andover, Mass.—William Austin graduated at Amherst College with the intention of entering the ministry, but while teaching in Williston Seminary, Easthampton, was attacked by typhoid fever, which terminated fatally Sept. 8, 1863. He was ill but a few days. The daughters, Ann S. and Laura M., were both successful teachers in the public schools for a number of years. Laura mar. Josiah H. Hunt, a native of Hawley, and removed to Gloucester, Mass., where her husband was for some years principal of one of the High Schools. Here she died Sept. 24, 1881, and her remains were brought here and laid beside those of her brother. The writer has her in grateful remembrance as a teacher for whom he had great admiration and respect and whom he firmly believed could not be excelled.

Austin, youngest son of James (1st) was educated for the ministry, graduating at Amherst College in 1824. Married Maria C. Odiorne of Boston, Dec. 12, 1827. Settled in New Hampshire, where he spent a long and useful life in that work.

JOSIAH SHAW.

Josiah Shaw settled in Plainfield in 1792. He was then an energetic young man of twenty-nine years. He had previously prospected and purchased a tract of land, and in February of that year, he with his wife and three young children made the journey from Abington. He served in

the Revolutionary army and is said to have carried a musket and fought at the battle of Bunker Hill, and to have been a sergeant at Saratoga and witnessed the surrender of Burgoyne; died Aug. 26. 1844, aged eighty-one. Children : Josiah, Jr. born in Abington, Nov. 13, 1785 ; Samuel, also born in Abington, May 6, 1790 ; Nancy, Feb. 4, 1794 ; Dana, April 10, 1798 ; Freeman, Feb. 23, 1803.
1. Josiah, Jr. mar. Lydia Noyes of Abington, died Dec. 13, 1863. Children : Louisa, born Nov. 27, 1808, died April 27, 1813 ; Mary Ann, born June 22, 1811 ; Washington, Jan. 11, 1814 ; Lewis, Nov. 3, 1816 ; Julia Ann, Oct. 25, 1818, died Oct. 3, 1850 ; Josiah, 3d, Oct. 3, 1820 ; Henry W., March 21, 1825 ; Eliza A., Aug. 29, 1827 ; Helen H., Nov. 22, 1829, died June 2, 1834.—Mary Ann mar. Elijah Warner, Jr., Jan. 11, 1844, died Dec. 24, 1888.— Washington studied medicine, married and settled in Haydenville, where he practised his profession until his decease, some thirty years since. Had one son, Henry W., now living in Springfield, Mass.—Lewis remained on the farm and cared for his father and mother. He remained single until after the death of his parents, when he mar. Rachel C. Tuller of Haydenville, Nov. 16, 1864. Was chosen one of the Selectmen in 1854, and served in that office eighteen years in all, being for a number of years Chairman of the Board, which position he held at his death, April 16, 1884. He also served three years on the School Committee, being elected in 1875. At a town meeting held soon after his decease, the following was adopted: "*Resolved*, that as citizens of Plainfield we express our high appreciation of his wise and faithful management of public affairs, and tender our sympathy to the widow and her family under this heavy bereavement." His children are

Carrie L., born Sept. 18, 1865; Mary E., July 3, 1875.—
Carrie mar. Lucian A. White, (second wife) Dec. 24,
1886.

Josiah, 3d, mar. Romina M. Streeter, Jan. 22, 1850.
They removed to Wisconsin, where they now reside.

Henry W. settled in Springfield, Mass., and afterward
in N. Y. City. He was twice married and deceased in
1890. Had one daughter, Sarah.

Eliza A. mar. John G. Sawyer of Albion, N. Y.,
June 27, 1855. He at present has the honor of representing his district in Congress.

2. Samuel, of whom a history is given under head of
"Physicians," mar. Sarah Snell Bryant, daughter of
Dr. Peter Bryant of Cummington, in 1821. She died Dec.
12, 1824, at the age of twenty-two. They had one daughter, Ellen T. Married Clark W. Mitchell, now of Dalton,
Mass., Aug. 3, 1842; died March 12, 1891, aged sixty-eight.
Samuel mar. for a second wife Elizabeth O. Clarke of
Northampton, Oct., 1830. Children : Samuel Francis,
born Sept. 7, 1833; Stella A., Dec. 13, 1835; Sarah G., Dec.
17, 1836; Charles Lyman, Feb. 7, 1842; Laura A., June
27, 1846.—Samuel F., of whom a brief history is given elsewhere, mar. Adelaide Roberts of Philadelphia, Oct. 27,
1877, died Dec. 7, 1884.—Laura A. mar. Dr. E. Darwin
Hudson, Jr., a physician of N. Y. City, Sept. 7, 1871. He
deceased two or three years since. The surviving members of the family reside in Astoria, N. Y., excepting during the summer, when they occupy the old homestead, the
ownership of which they still retain.

3. Nancy mar. Edmund Campbell, May 23, 1817,
died Nov., 1820.

4. Dana mar. Elizabeth Whiton, April 2, 1829. He

was also a physician and practiced for more than twenty-five years in Barre, N. Y.; deceased many years since.

5. Freeman remained on the old homestead where his father first settled. Married Harriet Whiton, Aug. 28, 1828, died Jan. 6, 1876. Children : Ann Zeruiah, born March 14, 1832 ; F. Eugene, Aug. 2, 1834, died Dec. 30, 1854; Harriet Augusta, Feb. 11, 1837; Theodore W., June 14, 1839; Chauncey C., May 20, 1841; Diantha H., March 25, 1843; Elna I., Sept. 6, 1849.—Zeruiah mar. Alden F. Pettengill of Cummington, Nov. 10, 1853.—Augusta mar. Ira W. Hamlen, July 7, 1858.—Theodore mar. Martha E. White, Oct. 12, 1862. Has for many years been employed at the U. S. Armory at Springfield. Children : Anna, born Sept. 1, 1872, died May 22, 1879; Etta and Harry.—Chauncey married, and died a few years since at Brooklyn, N. Y. Theodore and Chauncey both served in the war of the Rebellion, Chauncey being the first volunteer from Plainfield.—Diantha mar. Joseph Woodward, Feb. 27, 1866.—Elna I. mar. Chas. C. Hall of Springfield, Oct. 1, 1868.

SAMUEL STREETER.

Samuel Streeter was a pioneer settler having come here while the town was a part of Cummington. He was born in Sturbridge, Mass., in 1754. After serving in the war of the Revolution he married Bathsheba Barton of Charlton in 1778, and settled where S. H. Sears now lives. Died Sept. 7, 1844, his wife having deceased six years before. Children : Hannah, born June 16, 1780; Joanna, Oct. 30, 1781, died Aug. 13, 1787; Jacob, Feb. 21, 1783; Susanna, July 30, 1785 ; Auselm, Oct. 4, 1787 ; Lucena, Jan. 4, 1789; Arnold, Oct. 14, 1790; Truman, Jan. 20, 1793; Samuel, Jr., Aug. 17, 1795 ; Nahum, Feb. 9, 1797.

1. Hannah mar. Timothy Barker of Heath, Aug. 19, 1802.

2. Jacob mar. Hannah Shaw Erskine, April 12, 1802. Children: Horace, born April 9, 1804, Almira, Jan. 30, 1806; Reed Erskine, Nov. 7, 1807; Betsey, June 25, 1809; Anna, Dec. 16, 1810, died Aug. 29, 1815; Jacob, Jr., April 2, 1812. This family removed to Ohio.

3. Susanna mar. Joel Carr, April 19, 1804.

5. Lucena mar. Ezra Beals, Jan. 29, 1807.

6. Arnold mar. Ruth Butler of Buckland, Nov., 1809, died May 8, 1872. Children: Romina, born 1810, died Oct. 2, 1812; Sereno, March 11, 1812, died Nov. 2, 1812; Sereno C., born in Pittsfield, Mass., April 22, 1814; Edwin P., June 3, 1816; Theron L., Aug. 17, 1818; Romina M., May 10, 1823; Ruth Ann, Feb. 6, 1828.—Sereno C. mar. Mercy Stetson. Children : Carrie A., born July 17, 1839; Belle G., April 11, 1843; Hiram C., May 8, 1849, died Sept. 9, 1850; George A., Sept. 15, 1852; Mary E., Nov. 22, 1854.—Carrie mar. J. Nelson Benjamin, Nov. 24, 1864.—Belle mar. Charles T. Estes of Adams, Dec. 13, 1874.—George mar. Vesta E. Whitmarsh, Dec. 24, 1873: Children: Cora M., born March 1, 1878; Edith L., Sept. 6, 1879; Herbert G., April 5, 1881. —Mary E. mar. Clarence Tower of Cummington, Oct. 29, 1878.

Edwin P. mar. Elsie Gloyd; died Nov. 18, 1888.

Theron L. mar. Maria B. Belding of Ashfield, Oct., 1845. Children: Clara M., born Oct. 4, 1846; Darwin E., March 27, 1848; William and Fred.

Romina M. mar. Josiah Shaw, 3d, Jan. 22, 1850.

Ruth Ann mar. George G. Keyes. Now reside in Delton, Wisconsin.

7. Truman, son of Samuel, mar. Nancy Hitchcock of Hawley, Sept. 1, 1817.
8. Samuel, Jr. mar. Anna Copeland, Aug. 30, 1820.
9. Nahum mar. Anna Butler, died Sept. 1, 1881. Children: Louisa, born July 19, 1824; Fred, Aug. 18, 1828; Lorenzo, Jan. 7, 1832; Julia Ann and Mary Ann, twins, Oct. 29, 1836.—Louisa mar. Solomon H. Deming, March 1, 1849.—Fred died in Greenfield, Mass., some years since.—Lorenzo served in the war of the Rebellion in the 37th Mass., and is now living in Vermont.—Julia A. mar. Chas. W. Bogart, Feb. 7, 1866. Live in Williamsburg, Mass.—Mary A. died Jan. 29, 1842.

JOSIAH TORREY.

Josiah Torrey was born in 1756, probably in Abington, Mass., and was without doubt a descendant of Capt. Wm. Torrey of Combe, St. Nicholas, County of Somerset, England, who came to this country in 1640 or '41 and settled in North Weymouth. This Capt. William was many times chosen representative to General Court. Was for about thirty years Clerk of the Courts of Norfolk County. He married his second wife after settling in Weymouth. The genealogy of Josiah is traced back as follows:—Josiah son of Josiah, of Phillip, of William, 2d, of Capt. William. His father was born in 1720, and settled in the west part of Abington. Josiah served in the Revolutionary war and as early as 1785 settled in Plainfield, on the farm now owned by C. W. Packard. He was called by the old people "Governor" Torrey, but how he obtained the title is not clear. The hill on which the house stands still bears his name. His wife died July 15, 1819. For a second he mar. Olive Segur, March, 1821. Died Aug. 6, 1836.

His children were John, Olive, Ruth, Nancy and Josiah, Jr., all of whom were probably born in Abington.—John mar. Betsey Colson, Oct., 1812.—Olive mar. Ansel Converse of Windsor, Nov., 1812.—Ruth mar. John Ford of Cummington, (second wife) May 18, 1834.—Nancy mar. Ebenezer Shaw, Jr. of Cummington, Jan. 2, 1817.—Josiah, Jr. mar. Polly Nash, Sept. 21, 1815. She died May 19, 1817. For a second wife he mar. Abigail Tirrell, widow of Isaac Tirrell, Jan., 1819. Their children were Mary N., born Sept. 27, 1819; Edwin T., Feb. 13, 1821; Philena L., Feb. 18, 1823; Merritt P., June 8, 1825; Austin W., Aug. 10, 1829; Francis N., Dec. 11, 1831.

1. Mary N. mar. Josiah Perkins. Reside in Pawtucket, R. I.

2. Edwin mar. Candace D. Stanford of Rowe, April, 1843. Children: Mary A., born 1844; George O., born Sept. 8, 1850, died Sept. 13, 1852; George A., Nov. 14, 1858.—Mary A. mar. James A. Nash, Sept. 15, 1860.— George A. mar. Philibena Stemple of Buckland, Jan. 21, 1883. Have one daughter, Mabel.

3. Philena, mar. William Gurney, (second wife) Jan., 1844.

4. Merritt mar. Celestia E. Tirrell, April 13, 1848. Was chosen one of the Selectmen in 1860 and served seven years. Also represented the town and district in the Legislature in 1877. Children: Flora L., born Sept. 20, 1856; Alden L., June 6, 1860.

5. Austin mar. Sarah L. J. Wing of Hinsdale, Mass., Oct., 1852.

6. Francis mar. Julia M. Remington, Nov. 24, 1853.

Austin and Francis were both teachers or School Superintendents in New Jersey for many years, being highly esteemed. Francis died a few years since from injuries received by being thrown from a wagon. His death was considered a great loss to the community in which he lived.

AMOS TIRRELL.

Amos Tirrell was born in Abington (or Weymouth) Mass., in 1763. Settled here about 1789, on the farm now occupied by Merritt Torrey. He was known by the name of "Old Orchard" among the towns-people. Presented each of his children on their marriage with a farm; died March 6, 1849. Children: Hannah, born in Abington, March 11, 1787; Isaac, Dec. 5, 1789; Amos, Jr., Nov. 18, 1792; Orren, June 13, 1795; Arza, Feb. 18, 1799; Abram Shaw, April 18, 1802; Clarissa, May 25, 1809, died July 12, 1825; James, Aug. 31, 1812.

1. Hannah mar. Samuel Thayer, Jr., March 27, 1806. Settled where Lemuel Mason now lives and reared a large family.

2. Isaac mar. Nabby Snow of Windsor, Feb., 1813, died Dec. 2, 1814; had one son who died in infancy.

3. Amos, Jr. mar. Electa Nash, March, 1813, died Nov. 16, 1825. Children: Russell, born Jan. 22, 1814; Lois J., Sept. 20, 1815; Isaac, Oct. 4, 1818; Sophronia, Aug. 13, 1820; Polly N., Aug. 2, 1823. His widow afterward mar. Benjamin Town.—Russell mar. Mrs. Lucy M. Campbell, widow of J. Dwight Campbell, April 22, 1852. Children: Arthur R., born Feb. 10, 1853; Emma L., June 26, 1857. —Arthur mar. Nellie M. Clark, Nov. 27, 1879.—Emma is a professional nurse in Hartford, Conn.

Lois J. mar. Daniel Burt of Southampton, Nov., 1834. Isaac mar. Melissa Sackett of Westfield. She deceased and he married his present wife who was Hannah Phipps. They reside in Holyoke.—Sophronia mar. Sumner Burt, April 21, 1840.—Polly N. mar. Edmund Burt of Southampton, June 12, 1850.

4. Orren mar. Lydia Snell of Ware, Aug. 5, 1817, died Jan. 25, 1880. Children: Sarah S., born 1819; Joseph W., Aug. 19, 1822; Orren, Jr., 1823; Mary C., Aug. 4, 1828, died Feb. 19, 1860; Emeline E., Aug. 9, 1830.—Sarah mar. Paul H. Cudworth, (second wife) Oct. 21, 1852.—Joseph W. mar. Huldah Woodard of Ware; has one son, Arthur W., a clergyman of the Methodist denomination, a promising young man. His wife deceased and for a second he mar. Antoinette C. Bryant of Chesterfield.—Orren, Jr. mar. Octavia Ford of Cummington, June 27, 1852.—Emeline mar. Edward Thayer of Chesterfield, Oct. 27, 1853.

5. Arza mar. Electa Snow. Children; Lydia P., born July 13, 1823; Artemas R., June 24, 1828; Susan G., Nov. 6, 1830; Elizabeth C., July 28, 1834; Spencer N., Jan. 27, 1838, and two who died in infancy.—Lydia mar. Justus Mason of Cummington, March 10, 1842; Artemas mar. Nancy Olds of Peru.—Susan mar. Brigham C. Streeter of Cummington, Oct., 1850.—Elizabeth mar. Spencer Tower of Chesterfield, Nov., 1852.—Spencer mar. for a second wife Samantha Haskins, April 7, 1864, who was a sister of his first.

6. Abram S. mar. Eunice Fuller, March 24, 1825, died Jan. 15, 1843. Children: Celestia E., born Jan. 25, 1828; Harriet A., Aug. 31, 1830; Elisha F., May 5, 1834, and one older daughter, who died in infancy.—Celestia mar. Merritt Torrey, April 13, 1848.—Harriet mar. Albert Ford of Windsor, May 9, 1850.

7. James mar. Clarissa Bird of Windsor, June, 1835; had two children who died in childhood, and adopted three.

ELIJAH WARNER.

Elijah Warner was born in Hardwick, Mass., in 1767. Mar. Betsey Mitchell of Cummington and settled on the farm afterwards occupied by his sons, Cushing and Wells. Was chosen one of the Selectmen in 1804 and served eighteen years. Represented the town in General Court at Boston in 1821 and 1827; was appointed a Justice of the Peace in 1828, and held the office until his death, which occurred Dec. 29, 1844. Children: Betsey, born Aug. 27, 1796; James, July 23, 1798; Melancia, July 8, 1800; Cushing, Sept. 16, 1802; William, Aug. 9, 1804; Elijah, Jr., Sept. 21, 1806; Wells, Dec. 12, 1808; Roswell H., Jan. 30, 1812; Janette, Sept. 20, 1819.

1. Betsey mar. Simeon Streeter of Cummington, (second wife) Dec. 23, 1830.

2. James mar. Fidelia Whiton, Sept. 23, 1824, died April 7, 1890. Children: James Emerson, born Sept. 24, 1825; Fidelia Loraine, Sept. 4, 1827; Florilla D., Feb. 11, 1830; Elizabeth R., April 3, 1832, died Dec. 8, 1834; Sarah W., Sept. 8, 1834; Almon M., March 6, 1843. J. Emerson became a physician and was for some years in California. At present resides in Sterling, Va.—F. Loraine mar. E. Alden Clark, Oct. 30, 1849, died Oct. 18, 1854.—Florilla D. mar. Alberto C. Shattuck, Jan. 1, 1852; he died Oct. 15 the same year. She afterwards mar. Rev. S. D. Taylor. They are now living at So. New Lyme, Ohio.—Sarah W. has been a teacher in the public schools of this and neighboring towns, having taught over fifty terms. She remained with her parents caring for them through their last years.

—Almon M. served three years in the war of the Rebellion in the 37th Mass., and was promoted to the rank of Lieut. Studied law and is now practising in Cincinnati, Ohio.

3. Melancia mar. Lemuel Howlett of Hartford, Ct. (third wife), April 26, 1853. Died in Plainfield, Nov. 3, 1884.

5. William mar. Annis Crittenden, April 23, 1835. Children : Wm. Edwards, born April 1, 1836 ; Eliza A., Sept. 11, 1837 ; Flora C., Jan. 29, 1840, died Dec. 14, 1841 ; Mary Flora, Sept. 24, 1842 ; Laura E., March 15, 1848. His wife died Oct. 30, 1852, and he mar. Mrs Polly P. Latham, widow of Robert A. Latham, Jan. 23, 1855. They had two children, twins, Frank A. and Fannie A., born Oct. 22, 1855. Frank died April 26, 1863. Wm. Edwards enlisted in the army in the fall of 1862, and served in the 46th Mass., which was stationed near Newbern, N. C., at which place he died while in the service, June 28, 1863, of typhoid fever. He was to have been married to Miss Augusta M. Dyer in the fall of 1862, had he not enlisted. It was thought best to postpone the marriage, which on account of his death never took place. Eliza A. mar. Wm. J. Shattuck (second wife). Reside in Covert, Mich.—Flora M. mar. Edward A. Rood, Oct. 25, 1863. They also reside at Covert, Mich.—Laura E. mar. George L. Campbell, Nov. 27, 1867. Reside in Northampton.—Fannie mar. Hiram Rood. Also live in Northampton.—William died Oct. 6, 1865.

6. Elijah, Jr. mar. Mary Ann Shaw, Jan. 11, 1844. Died Aug. 11, 1889. No children.

8. Roswell H. married and lived in Dalton, Mass. Died in 1890. Neither wife or children survive him. Cushing, Wells and Janette never married, but remained

on the old homestead. Cushing died May 2, 1882, and Wells died eight days later. It is a singular fact that it has been the lot of Janette to care for four of her brothers during their last sickness, viz.: Cushing, Wells, Elijah Jr., and Roswell, which she has done with great patience and faithfulness. She now resides in town with her nephew, C. W. Streeter.

CALEB WHITE.

Caleb White was one of the pioneer settlers. Came here while the district was still a part of Cummington, and lived in a house which stood a few rods south of the one occupied afterward by his son Samuel. Was born in Bridgewater, Mass., in 1744. Served in the Revolutionary army, being over thirty years old when the war commenced. A wooden flask or canteen which he carried in the service, is now in the possession of his great-granddaughter, Mrs. Theodore W. Shaw of Springfield, Mass. It bears the name of Caleb White, with date of May 9, 1775. He was chosen one of the selectmen the next year after Plainfield was set off, and served four years. He understood surveying and owned a surveyor's compass and other instruments, his services being often in demand. He died on the farm where he orignally settled, April 8, 1840, at the age of ninety-six. Had two sons. Ziba, born in Bridgewater, probably in 1771, and Samuel, born in Cummington, Sept. 16, 1776. Ziba lived on or near the spot where W. E. Shaw lives. Married Huldah Gloyd, Feb. 24, 1794, died April 6, 1842. Children: Hannah, born Oct. 25, 1797; Electa, April 26, 1799, both of whom died in early childhood. Nahum, Dec. 20, 1800; Loren, July 1, 1802; Calvin, Aug. 12,

1804; Amy, March 8, 1806; Newell, Nov. 30, 1807; Dexter, Nov. 17, 1809; Huldah, 1814. Loren mar. Harriet Beals, March 31, 1823.

Newell studied medicine, became a physician and settled in Pennsylvania, where he is still living.—Dexter mar. Lydia Gurney, Nov., 1837. Children: Dexter Wellington, born Jan. 4, 1839; Shepard L., Dec. 21, 1840; Mary Ellen, Nov. 3, 1844; Herbert H., Oct. 11, 1852.— Huldah mar. Wm. Gurney, June 8, 1836, died Aug. 1, 1842.

Samuel, son of Caleb, mar. Polly Norton, Nov. 28, 1799. Was chosen one of the selectmen in 1834 and served four years. Died March 21, 1871. Children: Norman, born Aug. 31, 1800; Mary, March 31, 1802; Annis, Feb. 4, 1804; Sally, Aug. 23, 1805; Deborah, June 1, 1807; William, Aug. 12, 1808; John, Jan. 21, 1810; Cynthia, March 19, 1812; Oren, Dec. 30, 1814; Samuel Orson, Jan. 12, 1817; Henry Kirke, March 31, 1820; Edwin T., Jan. 16, 1822, died Aug. 9, 1830; Armelia, Aug. 12, 1823; Brackley C., May 6, 1825, died Aug. 5, 1830. Three others, two sons and a daughter, died in infancy, making seventeen children in all, ten sons and seven daughters. This is believed to be the largest family ever produced in Plainfield. Norman mar. Albina Gloyd, June 20, 1821.—Mary mar. Vinson Nash, Dec. 5, 1821. He having deceased, she mar. Bela Dyer (third wife), June 2, 1865.—Annis mar. Orren Stetson, Jan. 1, 1828, Died March 10, 1885.—Sally mar. Levi Stetson, 2d, Feb. 12, 1824.—Deborah mar. Bela Dyer, Sept. 30, 1824, died Nov. 16, 1828.—William married and died Sept. 2, 1852.— Oren mar. Esther Wagner of Cummington, May, 1837.— Samuel O. (or Orson S. as he has always been known), mar. Louisa B. Shaw, daughter of David, Feb. 14, 1839, died Feb. 5, 1891. Had one daughter, Martha E., born Sept. 18, 1843, mar. Theodore W. Shaw, Oct. 12, 1862.—Also an adopted son, Lucian A.—Henry K. mar. Harriet N. Hastings of Buckland, Nov., 1841.—Armelia mar. Abner Gurney, Nov. 14, 1843. Only one of these sons, Orson S., settled in Plainfield.

DAVID WHITON.

David Whiton (this name has since been written Whiting) was one of the early settlers. His house stood where No. 2 school-house now stands. He was the son of Abijah and was born in Hingham, Mass., Nov. 10, 1769. Mar. Rachel Randall of Hatfield, (who was through her mother a descendant of Robert Bruce of Scotland,) Jan. 1795. He was a man of good executive ability and was often moderator of the town meetings. Died Sept. 9, 1849. Children: Mary, born Nov. 28, 1796; Fidelia, Dec. 27, 1799; Betsey, Dec. 22, 1801; David Randall, Feb. 6, 1803; Theodore, March 26, 1805; Harriet, May 18, 1807; Clarissa, Jan. 21, 1810; Rachel, Oct. 9, 1811; William Chandler. Feb. 10, 1813; Lewis E., March 7, 1815.—Mary mar. James Joy, June 10, 1818, died April 12, 1888.—Fidelia mar. James Warner, Sept. 23, 1824, died Aug. 11, 1887.—Betsey (or Elizabeth) mar. Dana Shaw, April 2, 1829.—David R. mar. Harriet Parker of Belchertown, Sept., 1832. Children: David Bruce, born Aug. 15, 1833; Theodore P., Jan. 28, 1836.—Harriet mar. Freeman Shaw, Aug. 28, 1828, died June 5, 1888.—Clarissa mar. Freeman Hamlen, died Oct. 13, 1847.—Rachel mar. Royal B. Hibbard of Barre, N. Y., May 27, 1835.—William C. mar. Lucretia Shaw, daughter of David, Oct. 30, 1836;

had one child, Wm. Augustus, born April 14, 1838, died Oct. 31, 1840. He is the only surviving member of the family.—Lewis E. mar. Diantha Shaw, and settled at Saratoga, N. Y. Died a few years since.

JACOB WHITMARSH.

Jacob Whitmarsh was born in Cummington, Jan. 1, 1789. Mar. Olive Packard, daughter of Adam Packard of Cummington, Dec. 29, 1814. She was a school-mate of Wm. Cullen Bryant. He used to say there was no competitor in his spelling class whom he feared except Olive Packard. They settled in the extreme southwest corner of the town, about a mile north of West Cummington, which at that time had no existence as a village. Died Feb. 9, 1872, his wife having deceased a few years before. Children: Polly P., born Nov. 19, 1815; Florintha, April 15, 1817; Mary Ann, Jan. 14, 1819; Jacob S., June 9, 1823; Fordyce, April 29, 1826; Rachel, May 21, 1831; Nahum, Oct. 16, 1834.

1. Polly mar. Robert A. Latham, May 24, 1838. Lived on the place lately occupied by Abishur Nash. Mr. Latham in company with Dea. Elias Giddings owned and operated a tannery near where Lester Streeter lives. He died July 23, 1851, leaving four children. For a second husband she mar. William Warner, Jan. 23, 1855. He died Oct. 6, 1865, and for a third she mar. Riley Westcott of Cheshire, about 1870. She died at Florence, Mass., Feb. 10, 1885.

2. Florintha mar. Verren Dawes of Cummington, May 24, 1837. He deceased leaving two small children, and about 1858 she mar. Isaac Bates of Cummington. He died about 1864, also leaving two small children. In April,

1871, she mar. Lewis Ford of Cleveland, Ohio, where they now reside.

3. Mary Ann mar. Newell Dyer, May 24, 1842, died May 2, 1866.

4. Jacob S. mar. Polly Bartlett of Cummington, Nov. 30, 1848. Children: Vesta, born 1851, and Alvah, and two who died in infancy.—Vesta mar. George A. Streeter, Dec. 24, 1873. They live on and have charge of the Wm. Cullen Bryant place in Cummington.—The wife of Jacob S. died in Worthington, and for a second he mar. Maria S. Nash, April 10, 1865. Children: Mattie P., born March 20, 1867; Bessie V., Sept. 28, 1872, died 1890. Reside in Florence, Mass. He was chosen one of the School Committee in 1871, serving three years; has also served on the School Board in other towns.

5. Fordyce mar. Eliza Allen of Windsor, Jan., 1852. Was chosen one of the Selectmen in 1858, serving two years. Children: Julia; Fannie A., born Nov. 7, 1857; Sarah A., Nov. 25, 1861.—Julia mar. J. H. Judd of Easthampton. Now reside in St. Paul, Minn.—Fannie mar. Granville Matthews. Reside in Chelsea, Mass.—Fordyce's wife deceased about 1886. For a second wife he mar. Mrs. Marion C. Dyer, widow of Edwin J. Dyer, Dec. 5, 1888. They reside in Easthampton, Mass.

6. Rachel mar. Levi N. Campbell, (second wife) Nov. 24, 1852. Died in Florence, Mass., Jan., 1887.

7. Nahum mar. Mary Lucas of Springfield, Nov. 1, 1871. Reside in Springfield, Mass.

www.ingramcontent.com/pod-product-compliance
Lightning Source LLC
Chambersburg PA
CBHW072129160426
43197CB00012B/2042